Make it happen!

By the same author:

Rapid Reading (Pan, 1988)
How to be a Rapid Reader (NTC Learning Works, 1991)
Beat the Bumph! (Nicholas Brealey, 1995)

Make it happen!

A step-by-step guide
from creativity to innovation

KATHRYN M. REDWAY

PIATKUS

Copyright © 2003 by Kathryn M. Redway

First published in 2003 by
Judy Piatkus (Publishers) Limited
5 Windmill Street
London W1T 2JA
e-mail: info@piatkus.co.uk

The moral right of the author has been asserted

A catalogue record for this book is available from the British Library

ISBN 0 7499 2388 1

Edited by Ian Paten
Text design by Briony Chappell, Goldust Design

Illustrated by Rodney Paull

This book has been printed on paper manufactured with respect for the environment using wood from managed sustainable resources

Typeset by Action Publishing Technology Ltd, Gloucester
Printed and bound in Great Britain by
MPG Books, Bodmin, Cornwall

Contents

Acknowledgements

Like innovation which cannot happen through a single person, so this book was not the product solely of my own mind. My work on this subject began in the mid-eighties when I had some luck in meeting influential people. I wish to thank these people now.

First, Norman Duncan, then an executive with Shell Oil advising the President, who demonstrated to me the importance of innovation for organisations. As our discussions multiplied, my own thinking began to take shape. This starting point was decisive.

Almost at the same time, I met Didier Gonin, then Director of Management Development at IBM Europe. He was the first to entrust me with testing some of my ideas on unsuspecting European managers. Didier left IBM and we continue to collaborate on some projects; in many ways he continues to be a mentor and I thank him.

Thank you also to Ivan Habanec who structured my own thinking and helped me design tools. I recall many lively dinners in my house when we tried some techniques on ourselves before launching them into organisations. The KR Questionnaire® is a good example.

Finally, this book would not have begun without the firm prodding of His Honour Peter Crawford QC who was the first to understand and visualise the final format. His judicious remarks migrated easily from the courtroom to these pages, for which I am very grateful.

Also, I was very lucky to find my publisher, in particular Gill Bailey, Editorial Director, who grasped instantly my aims in this book. Her editorial team helped the book come to fruition and gave me excellent advice.

This book is dedicated to my husband, Keith, who was involved in its various incarnations.

Preface

Over the last 20 years I have worked with thousands of people in organisations who strive to innovate. Many UK businesses, large and small, recognise that to survive and prosper they need to challenge the status quo, break down established thinking patterns, look across boundaries and make connections; in short, they need to violate the rules and procedures they have created. No doubt, as a manager, you will have been in a situation when you have exhorted your team to try something new only to find your own boss sceptical about taking a risk. Or perhaps, during a critical time in the development of your new idea, you ran into problems that no one had considered, or discovered that, towards the implementation stage, people were moved, or everyone around you got cold feet and you had to carry out the final stages on your own.

This book is aimed at managers at every level and will show you how to overcome these hurdles. It will explain how to manage the process of innovation. It will show you that it is possible to pursue a positive strategy to foster innovation.

WHAT IS INNOVATION?

You cannot recognise innovation, foster it or manage it unless you understand what it truly is. The innovative process is simply the putting together of known elements in a different way to meet a newly defined need, whether

x   Make it happen!

this need is a new product, a new process, a new service or a better way of carrying out an old procedure.

Many businesspeople think that innovation in their company will require an elaborate programme of research and development or the acquisition of expensive technology. While these have their place, most new business ideas, new ways to compete and many new products are not driven by new technology. They are found by searching systematically for ways to improve your internal processes and the delivery of your service or products, and by responding better to your customers' needs. This is something every business and every organisation can do if it puts its collective mind to it. Innovation is *not* just for technical types but for everyone in the organisation. If you have been taught to innovate, you too can *Make it Happen!*

HOW THIS BOOK IS ORGANISED

All innovations progress through three steps:

Idea + Development + Implementation = Innovation

This book is organised following these steps. Part 1 is about **Ideas**, how to generate them and harness them systematically. In this section you will acquire the skills to expand your creative abilities, will be given tools for generating ideas and focusing on opportunities, will be shown how to select an idea from a variety of potentially valid ones, will be shown the disciplines involved in writing a business plan, and will be given the opportunity to brush up on your skills of presentation and persuasion.

Part 2, on **Development**, focuses on making the idea fit for the purpose. In this section you will be presented with the tools to get your ideas off the ground, will be told at what stage to involve your customers and senior management, and will be reminded that failures and setbacks abound and shown how to deal with them.

Part 3 deals with **Implementation** – the proof of the pudding, the reality, the success. In this section you will be reminded that innovations rarely turn out exactly as planned and will be shown how to deal with this, will be warned about the delicate early stages of implementation and will be given the tools to deal with these, will be shown how to increase your customer base while keeping a watchful eye on competitors, will be encouraged to welcome discontinuity, and will be offered ideas on how to reward and give recognition to your team.

Each part is divided into short chapters which can be dipped into independently of the others. They are designed to help you, the innovator, when you are stuck at any stage in the process. Treat this book as you would a car maintenance manual: go to the section and chapter you need. Practical case studies at the end of some chapters illustrate how other organisations have used and interpreted the ideas offered.

We start with an Introduction which concentrates on you, the reader, asks you some questions to help you assess yourself in the context of innovation, and shows you how to spot the difference between a creative and an innovative person, and how to measure to what extent you are working in an environment conducive to your innovative aspirations.

Introduction:
Knowing myself and my environment

Chapter 1
How creative am I?

'Creative minds always have been known to survive any kind of bad training.'
– ANNA FREUD, CHILD PSYCHOLOGIST

'The very essence of the creative is its novelty, and hence we have no standard by which to judge it.'
– CARL R. ROGERS, PSYCHOTHERAPIST

'You see things; and you say "Why". But I dream things that never were; and say "Why not?"'
– GEORGE BERNARD SHAW, DRAMATIST

This first chapter is perhaps the most controversial, for the simple reason that there are so many myths about creativity, making it hard to define.

First, let's reflect on Isaac Newton's remark *'If I have seen further, it is by standing on the shoulders of giants'*. He suggests that his own creative powers would not have been possible without the work of others. In other words the creative process does not happen in a vacuum but is the product of a society, or culture. Put bluntly, creativity is not magic, an 'out of nowhere' kind of chance happening. In his 1964 book *The Act of Creation* Arthur Koestler was the first to recognise that the creative act 'uncovers, selects, reshuffles, combines, synthesises already existing facts, ideas, faculties, skills'. He proposed that in order to create something new, one needs to break old thinking patterns and form new ones. Or to put it a slightly different way, the creative process is about making so far unrecognised connections. Easier said than done, I hear you say!

ARE YOU CREATIVE?

How do we recognise creativity? Think of half a dozen people you believe to be creative – whether people around you or perhaps giants like Leonardo da Vinci, Frank Whittle or Alexander Fleming.

What characteristics or abilities do these people have in common which make them creative? Note down a dozen that they all share. Obvious abilities with which you could start your list might include:

- Thinking imaginatively
- Solving problems in a different way from normal
- Seeing possibilities others have not
- Initiating change

Now, how many of the abilities you have written down do you honestly believe you have? If you display some of these characteristics, you are probably creative; if not you may be innovative (see Chapter 2). But perhaps if you do not recognise yourself as creative or innovative you can play a role in nurturing and guiding such types. You may well have a talent for organising and administering.

LOGIC OR CREATIVITY?

Does logic or creativity predominate in your character? The logical person tends to analyse or synthesise another's work and draw conclusions in a single, sequential mode of thinking. Creative thinking, on the other hand, is a process associated with intuition, insight, originality – even motivation and knowledge. To be creative, you need to develop attitudes that are conducive to creative thinking – for example, an attitude whereby you encourage yourself to search for ideas and to manipulate your knowledge to open up new possibilities. We learn by accumulating experiences which we group into patterns and refer back to later. We become creative when we relate things or ideas which were previously unrelated. Koestler coined the phrase 'bisociative thinking' to explain creativity. He postulated that when the mind searches for the answer to a problem it starts on one plane and wanders on until another plane – or term of reference – is met. On the face of it, the two planes are unrelated, but later a link is seen with the solution to the problem. In humour, an example of creative thinking, the laughter produced at the end of a joke marks the release of tension that accompanies the act of creation. Tension and frustration are often a prelude to creation.

SOME CREATIVE CHARACTERISTICS

The creative person usually enjoys problem-solving and tends to bring fresh perspectives to old problems. He or she is prepared to abandon the way things have always been done and introduce or embrace new practices. He or she is aware of changes in the environment that may alter things, thinks about what may happen in the future and keeps an open mind.

 Try this

Ponder the following questions:

→ Do you like problems?

→ Do you let your mind wander and embrace 'blue sky' thinking?

→ Do you enjoy new experiences?

→ Do you find that in meetings you have several ways of dealing with the problems others are discussing?

→ Do you enjoy being around people with a sense of humour?

→ Do you tend to see things others have not yet noticed?

 In practice

To encourage your creative abilities, you might like to try the following:

1. During meetings, defer judgement on a new idea.
2. Talk about the positive aspects of an idea before subjecting it to critical thinking.
3. Give yourself a few minutes of thinking time during the day. Keep a diary of the thoughts you have during these periods.
4. Read about creativity techniques, try them and keep a record of what works best for you.
5. Make a list of the people around you who you think are creative. Observe them and emulate some of their behaviour.

Further resources

Hofstadter, Douglas R., *Metamagical Themas*, Penguin (1985), in particular Chapter 12.

Koestler, Arthur, *The Act of Creation*, Picador (1964).

Minsky, Marvin, *The Society of Mind*, Simon & Schuster (1986), in particular Chapters 6.86, 11, 13.1 and 18.4.

Chapter 2
How innovative am I?

*Akio Morita's Sony Walkman originated in his wish to
listen to music while playing tennis. He overcame design
difficulties with determination, showing his employees a
brick and urging them to make the device a similar size.
When they succeeded he showed them a pocket book
and said, 'Smaller still.' Sony employees achieved it.*

List ten innovations in, for instance, services, products,
government, society, technology or communications that
have affected you in the last ten years or so. Make a second
list of innovations that you or any of your colleagues have
introduced in the last ten years or so.

In the first list you may have included the mobile phone,
e-mail, Peps and Isas, grocers selling petrol, or PCs in the
classroom.

In terms of the second list, concentrate now on what
made you or your colleagues successful. Was it tenacity, a
gap in the market, the desire to succeed with an end
product, knowledge, patience, frustration, or hard work?

This will help you understand what innovation is –
namely, 'a novel idea, developed and successfully implemented'. To paraphrase management consultant Peter
Drucker, an innovation is measured by 'its impact on the
environment'.

HOW DOES INNOVATION DIFFER FROM CREATIVITY?

In Chapter 1 we looked at how creative people make connections. Innovators not only make connections, they see – almost simultaneously – whether any new idea is useful, whether it fills a gap. The major difference between creative and innovative people is that innovators are interested in a result. Creative people do not need this: what motivates them, what gives them a kick, is the idea, the connection they have made. Successful implementation does not worry them. It does worry innovators.

Do I detect scepticism? Well, let me illustrate. Sir Clive Sinclair is a creative individual, but success in the marketplace is not his motivation. What turns him on is having new ideas – plenty of them – whether or not people find them useful. The C5 vehicle that he devised about 20 years ago is the epitome of this syndrome. The concept of a small, pollution-free mode of transport was not in tune with an era when people, at least in Europe and North America, were flaunting their wealth. Sinclair did not check out the market need for the C5. Furthermore, the device experienced some stability problems – in other words, the technology was a little dodgy.

Compare this to the case of James Dyson. He understood that people were getting tired of Hoover, who had not changed their products for decades. He also made a different connection, coming up with technology that bypassed the need to replace bags. I am a housewife: the idea appealed, and when I needed to change my vacuum cleaner I chose Dyson.

So what lessons have we learned? Quite a few.

1. Innovation cannot happen unless someone, somewhere, has a creative mind and first makes the new connection.
2. Innovation needs a commercial motivation – that

is, success in the marketplace. Without commercial success you have a failed idea (which can, however, be revived when the time is right).

3. Innovation is hard work, as it goes beyond having ideas. It requires a focused mind. Part 2 of this book is about how to turn a novel, interesting idea into an innovation.

4. In organisations you cannot achieve innovation alone – unlike the purely creative types who are content to think unencumbered by systems and bureaucracy. You need a sponsor who will help you to success.

5. Timing is important in innovation. Leonardo da Vinci was creative but not innovative because he did not have the means to test his flying machine.

6. Some people are both creative and innovative. But they are rare!

SOME INNOVATIVE CHARACTERISTICS

To check whether you have innovative abilities and desires, see to what extent you agree with the following statements.

- I usually like new and creative ideas
- I like to test new ideas to see whether they will work
- I know people with whom I can discuss new ideas
- I am tenacious and persistent
- I can anticipate obstacles that may hinder the development or implementation of an idea
- I am able to obtain help
- I learn from past successes and failures
- I like to cut through red tape, bureaucratic rules and procedures
- I know which rules I must obey and those that may be bent
- I can carry on even if I am isolated

Notice that the above list of innovative characteristics differs from that for creativity by its emphasis on a desire and a willingness to strive for success.

ARE YOU WORKING FOR AN INNOVATIVE ORGANISATION?

If the majority of the following statements are correct for the organisation you work in, then it is an innovative organisation (the next chapter measures this more rigorously):

- Management encourage employees to take initiatives
- Management uses measurements to accept risks
- Company vision may go beyond plans
- Achievement is more important than plans
- Finding better ways of working is preferred to sticking to procedures
- People are encouraged to take responsibility for their decisions, not to pass the buck
- Relationships are informal, cross-functional, not hierarchical
- Change is used as an opportunity for advantage
- Individual freedom and autonomy are valued above promotion and money
- Creativity and innovation are rewarded
- Mistakes are used to learn, not hidden or punished

Case study

In the 1890s gunfire from ships was pretty inaccurate. The gun, in a fixed position on the ship, which was probably rolling from side to side and pitching from stem to stern, made scoring a 'hit' on the target a matter of luck. Admiral Sir Percy Scott, RN, had realised that continuously moving the gun barrel back and forth, in a direction opposite to the movement of the ship, made accuracy much more likely. It was in the Far East that Scott met William Sims, a junior United States Navy officer. The men took a liking to each other – both were choleric, intolerant of spit-and-polish, and had a contempt for bureaucratic inefficiency. Sims took to Scott's ideas, and modified some of the guns on his ship, the USS *Kentucky*, with the Englishman's help. This led to Sims' complete conversion to continuous-aim firing, and he produced 13 official reports recommending changes in the then standard and ineffective gun-laying method. His first reports were rebutted – US equipment was just as good as its British counterpart – and Sims' results were proved 'wrong' by tests made on dry land. It was not until Sims wrote to the President of the United States, Teddy Roosevelt, that any action was taken on his and Scott's ideas and they were adopted by the US Navy.

This story illustrates how innovation needs an environment ready for change and a mind ready to recognise the possibilities for improvement, how some unimaginative people will oppose change, and the need for an imaginative sponsor.

Further resources

Morison, Elting E., *Men, Machines, and Modern Times*, MIT Press (1966).

Chapter 3
The KR questionnaire®

Consider these questions:
- What attracts people to your organisation?
- What makes people leave your organisation?

The following questionnaire assesses the extent to which your personal goals and the goals of your organisation coincide, with an emphasis on the areas of innovation and individual creativity. By completing it you will consider your own leaning towards innovation, and to what extent your organisation constrains or supports your goals.

Read through the following statements, applying them to you and the organisation you work for. Then circle a number: 1 if you strongly agree with the statement, 2 if you agree, 4 if you disagree, and 5 if you strongly disagree. Use 3 if you neither agree nor disagree and for 'don't know'.

Relate your answers to your personal beliefs in terms of your position within your organisation. Redefine the word 'department' if another, such as 'section' or 'group', is more meaningful to you.

1. The policies and procedures are strictly set and observed to prevent excesses

    1   2   3   4   5

2.   Work should be interesting and exciting
     1   2   3   4   5

3.   Pleasing the boss is more important for one's career
     than competence
     1   2   3   4   5

4.   After years of experience management believes that
     department policies and procedures express the
     most efficient practices
     1   2   3   4   5

5.   A challenge at work adds spice to it
     1   2   3   4   5

6.   Management should encourage staff to suggest ideas
     for changes in the ways the department works
     1   2   3   4   5

7.   Only after plans and budgets are approved can a
     project start
     1   2   3   4   5

8.   Our organisation works like clockwork
     1   2   3   4   5

9.   Making a good impression on senior managers is
     more important for one's career than being good at
     one's job
     1   2   3   4   5

10. Channels of communication are clearly defined and
     adhered to
     1   2   3   4   5

11. I enjoy the company of my colleagues
    1   2   3   4   5

12. Even staff who are loyal or competent should not have a job for life
    1   2   3   4   5

13. Making a mistake is not easily forgiven
    1   2   3   4   5

14. Employment is very important for the majority of staff
    1   2   3   4   5

15. Clear and measurable standards of performance are used for employee evaluation
    1   2   3   4   5

16. Many staff feel trapped in the department and its systems
    1   2   3   4   5

17. Central departments, e.g. Management, Accounts, Administration, have responsibility for innovations
    1   2   3   4   5

18. There is hardly any team spirit in the department
    1   2   3   4   5

19. Senior management believes that the level of success it achieves is a measure of its own worth
    1   2   3   4   5

20. Senior management treats staff as disposable resources
    1   2   3   4   5

21. When it comes to the crunch, pleasing senior management is the most important factor in making decisions

    1   2   3   4   5

22. Managers should be helpers, not just order-givers

    1   2   3   4   5

23. Remuneration and benefits should form a flexible system geared to individual performance

    1   2   3   4   5

24. In spite of staff journals and other departmental media, most staff have no idea what is going on in the department or in the company generally

    1   2   3   4   5

25. 'Rocking the boat' can endanger staff prospects

    1   2   3   4   5

26. Most staff want additional responsibilities as soon as they are capable of carrying them out

    1   2   3   4   5

27. Most staff do not need clear-cut directions from their superior to do their jobs

    1   2   3   4   5

28. The workload is usually even and predictable

    1   2   3   4   5

29. Professionals/specialists need a substantial amount of freedom to do their job best

    1   2   3   4   5

30. The remuneration system should be applied equally to every member of staff
1   2   3   4   5

31. Policies and departmental interests have priority over an individual's considerations
1   2   3   4   5

32. Informal contacts across boundaries are discouraged (both within and between departments)
1   2   3   4   5

33. There is a clear-cut career progression system within our organisation
1   2   3   4   5

34. I want to be treated as an individual, not a number
1   2   3   4   5

35. Management tries to ensure that there are standards and guidelines for every eventuality
1   2   3   4   5

36. I dislike the idea of my life being planned for me by someone else
1   2   3   4   5

37. Flexible working hours increase productivity and staff motivation
1   2   3   4   5

38. The work is so organised that every staff member knows what he/she is supposed to do
1   2   3   4   5

39. Having a clear conscience and peace of mind is very
    important to me
    1   2   3   4   5

40. Job descriptions make sure that there are no gaps or
    overlaps in individual duties
    1   2   3   4   5

41. Special assignments outside one's normal job are
    necessary for personal growth
    1   2   3   4   5

42. In normal circumstances most people try to do their
    best
    1   2   3   4   5

43. Staff have the right to know what's happening in the
    department
    1   2   3   4   5

44. Imagination and creativity are important qualities
    for senior staff
    1   2   3   4   5

45. There is more competition than cooperation
    between departments within the organisation
    1   2   3   4   5

ANALYSING THE RESULTS

To assess your individual score, add all those numbers (1
to 5) you have circled for questions 2, 5, 6, 11, 14, 22, 23,
26, 27, 29, 34, 36, 37, 39, 41, 42, 43, 44. The score for the
organisation is the sum of all the remaining numbers. The
sum of numbers for an individual (A score) falls between

18 and 90 (inclusive), while the total for an organisation (B score) must fall between 27 and 135 (inclusive).

The probability of the individual and organisation succeeding is determined by the ratio

$$\frac{\text{Organisation score}}{\text{Individual's score}}$$

A value for organisation/individual of 1.5 indicates an 'average' position. Values greater than 1.5 indicate that you or the department are pushing for improvement.

Mark the two scores on the following diagram to determine your position in your organisation. If the result appears to the right of and above the diagonal line, this indicates some degree of innovation; below it and to the left indicates an atmosphere unconducive to innovation.

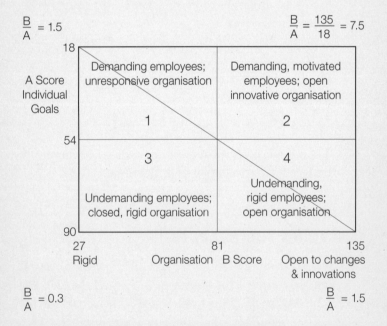

The KR Questionnaire® – analysing the results

The best score falls into Box 2. In this situation the employee's needs and what the organisation needs often dovetail neatly.

In Box 1, we have employees with high expectations who can offer the organisation the seeds of renewal. Unfortunately the organisation is unresponsive: it does not understand the needs or the potential of its employees or is unable to change its structure.

In Box 4 the organisation has recruited – or retained – the wrong people. It is a rare occurrence but does occasionally happen.

In Box 3 the future is bleak: neither employees nor organisation has the capacity for innovation or self-renewal.

Part 1:
Ideas – generating the concept

Chapter 4
Visualisation – creating your inner picture

'Genius consists in seeing what everyone has seen and thinking what no one thought.'
– ALBERT SZENT-GYÖRGYI, NOBEL PRIZE-WINNING BIOCHEMIST

'Imagination was given to man to compensate him for what he is not. A sense of humour was provided to console him for what he is.'
– HORACE WALPOLE, ENGLISH WRITER AND CONNOISSEUR

You were born with imagination. Visualisation involves manipulating it, recreating images that can be used to illustrate abstract concepts, and forms an essential part of other techniques, for example lateral thinking and the use of metaphors.

Think for a moment of great achievers: they all use visualisation to accomplish their goal. Muhammad Ali visualised when he would knock out his opponent during a boxing match; Einstein visualised himself travelling on a sunbeam into the universe and 'felt' his theory of relativity; Friedrich von Kekulé – the father of organic chemistry – 'saw' the flames of a fire becoming a snake swallowing its own tail, which gave him the idea for the formula for benzene; Mary Shelley visualised modern-day spare-parts surgery when her hero, Frankenstein, constructed a human form from fragments of bodies. These people are driven by a clear picture in their minds of what they want to achieve.

Creative and innovative people have learned to use visualisation. They sense and see ahead of others what is needed.

RECONNECT WITH YOUR ENVIRONMENT

Visualisation is complex because it relies on our ability to recreate images and to create at will relevant images from the virtually unlimited material stored in the mind.

So, first you need to *see*. Because we are saturated with information, we do not see, or take in, information properly. We assume we already know what we need to know. You can learn to do better through conscious effort. Try this simple test: close your eyes and recreate lunch last Sunday. Can you smell the food? Is the taste of it definable? Who were your lunch companions? What did they wear? Train yourself – once every day look around in a specific place, either going to work, in a meeting or in a room at home. Take in the information in detail and exercise your senses. Does this colour please you? Is this shape attractive? Are you aware of any smell? Now, averting or closing your eyes, can you recreate what you have seen? Check your accuracy.

When you have sharpened your ability to connect with your environment, you can use it in other, creative ways. For example, close your eyes: can you imagine an elderly person you know well changing back into a teenager?

In his remarkable book *The Seven Habits of Highly Effective People*, Stephen R. Covey invites the reader to his or her own funeral. He asks what they would like people to say about them, what contributions or achievements, what trait of character, they should single out. He calls it 'Begin with an end in mind'. In other words, before physical creation there is mental creation.

 Try this

When a managing director comes to me with problems relating to their business, I ask them to write down on one sheet of A4 what they want to leave behind three or five years from now. What kind of customer do they want? With regard to the competition, where do they see their company positioned? At a local or European level, how far do they see the company expanding? What sort of employees do they need? And so on. Although most find the task difficult, as they reflect on these issues the picture they form in their mind helps them focus on what they want to do and how they will achieve it.

 In practice

To exercise your imagination and visualisation skills, try the following:

Think of each of the items listed below, and then write C for clear, V for vague and N for nothing after each, according to how sharp the image or sensation appears in your mind.

1. The face of a friend
2. The grille on the front of your car
3. A camellia blossom
4. The earth from orbit
5. A friend's laugh
6. The feel of wet grass
7. The sensation of a long attack of hiccups

Did you find some images more difficult to recreate? Practise those for which you wrote V and N until they become clear.

Once you feel comfortable with the technique of visualising, tackle gradually more complex situations, perhaps beginning with your view of a competitor in your market. For example, can you see your product dominating the shelf display in a shop while your competitor's product is small, dark and difficult to find? As you generate images about the situation you will see it from many possible standpoints, and by working in a conceptual framework you can weigh up a range of different perspectives on a given problem or situation.

Further resources

Adams, James L., *Conceptual Blockbusting*, Addison-Wesley (1986), in particular pp. 88–95.

Covey, Stephen R., *The Seven Habits of Highly Effective People*, Simon & Schuster (1992), in particular pp. 98–144.

Fritz, Robert, *Creating*, Butterworth/Heinemann (1991), in particular pp. 25–6 and 174.

Gawain, Shakti, *Creative Visualization*, New World Library (1995).

Chapter 5
Shall I compare thee – using metaphors and similes

'Shall I compare thee to a summer's day?'
– WILLIAM SHAKESPEARE

A metaphor is a figure of speech whereby something is spoken of in terms of what it resembles, whereas in a simile a person or thing is explicitly likened to another, usually preceded by the words 'as' or 'like'. You could call them analogies. The aim of using metaphors and similes is to find similarities between unrelated situations.

HOW OTHERS HAVE USED METAPHORS

Metaphors and similes have been used for a long time; Jesus Christ taught in parables, which are metaphors wrapped up in a story. The Book of Proverbs uses them extensively. For example, *'who boasts himself of a false gift is like clouds and wind without rain'* (25:14), or *'The fear of the king is as the roaring of a lion'* (20:2).

Look at other people's ways of expressing an abstract concept. This is American statesman Benjamin Franklin:

'A man without a goal is like shooting a gun without a target.' Or psychiatrist C. G. Jung: *'The meeting of two personalities is like the contact of two chemical substances: if there is any reaction, both are transformed.'* And one of my favourites, from author Alec Waugh: *'For nine-tenths of the year London life, with its noise and colour and animation, is like a story by Dostoevsky. In August it is like a story by Turgenev, still and calm and deep.'*

Have you ever come across the concept of the invisible monkey clinging to one's shoulder in the context of time management? This metaphor was introduced by American management guru William Oncken to illustrate how, when someone approaches you with the opening gambit 'Have you got a minute?', he has an invisible monkey on his shoulder that he wants to transfer to yours. Oncken's suggestion is that you make sure the monkey stays where it is!

METAPHOR AND SIMILE IN DAILY LIFE

Don't you sometimes say 'My heart is pumping', 'Your batteries have gone dead' or 'Some ideas are half baked'? Notice that everyday metaphors rely on visualising objects. When I was at school, learning German, the teacher gave us this rule to learn the declensions of German adjectives preceded by the articles *der*, *die*, *das*. 'Think of it as a gun,' she said. In the nominative all three genders end in **e** and in the accusative the feminine and neuter also end in **e**. (In all other cases the ending is –**en**.) The picture looks like this:

Nominative	der gut-e	die gut-e	das gut-e
Accusative		die gut-e	das gut-e

Strip out the words, and the picture becomes:

e e e
  e e

The shape of a gun! Forty years on, I still remember.

 Try this

Let us look at an example. Imagine that you are faced with a colleague who refuses to do a particular task because it is not in her job description, even though she has the time to do it. You have reached deadlock. To resolve this situation, use a metaphor. Is it not similar to dealing with a child? Note the similarities:

→ They both may want praise or a reward
→ They both may want the freedom to do what you ask in the way they want
→ They both may want serious negotiation leading to a compromise
→ They both may need reassurance or training
→ They may both be bored by the prospect of what you are asking them to do

By examining every avenue, you may gain fresh insight into the problem and how to overcome it.

When faced with problems, try inviting a couple of colleagues to discuss the situation with you, and practise using metaphors or similes. Find another situation you could compare this one to – ask yourself, 'What does this remind me of?' Let the associations form, then see if there is any overlap with your current problem.

In practice

A metaphor works well when you are:

➜ Facing a complex problem. The picture will become clearer (another metaphor!) if you compare the problem with a more familiar situation.

➜ Warming up for brainstorming.

Seek out people who are gifted in using examples, stories and experiences while conveying complex or abstract information. Listen to them and learn from them.

Try the following, alone or with others. Visualise and jot down how:

➜ Cooking a meal is like driving a car
➜ Giving a speech is like having a baby
➜ Making a sales call is like writing a story
➜ Managing a project is like planting a garden

For example, you need to plan your meal, just as you need to plan where you are going – your route – when driving.

Further resources

Michalko, Michael, *Thinkertoys*, Ten Speed Press (1991), in particular Chapter 25.

Petty, Geoffrey, *How to Be Better at Creativity*, Kogan Page (1997), in particular Chapter 4.

Von Oech, Roger, *A Kick in the Seat of the Pants*, Harper & Row (1986), in particular pp. 72–6.

Chapter 6
Establishing connections – Mindmaps®

*'Some painters transform the sun into a yellow spot,
others form a yellow spot in the sun.'*
– PABLO PICASSO, ARTIST

*'Discovery consists of looking at the same thing as every-
one else and thinking something different.'*
– ALBERT SZENT-GYÖRGYI, NOBEL PRIZE-WINNER

We are all used to situations when we jot down a few
ideas, whether to clarify our thinking on a specific issue or
in preparation for giving a presentation. Many of us note
down our ideas in a list format. Lists have their uses, but
they fail to stimulate the brain's creativity. As an example,
consider the subject of holidays. Imagine that you are planning a holiday but are not entirely sure where to go and
what to do, so you start a list. It might include:

Weather	Cost
Package	New experience
Practise French	City
Beach	Swimming
Go back to X	Europe

| Relax | Visit something |
| Go with X | Visit friends |

This explores the options available to you, but how are you going to make a decision? Try a Mindmap®.

 Try this

Invented about 30 years ago by learning expert Tony Buzan, the Mindmap® is a non-linear technique for making notes. It is visual and allows you to connect ideas.

To generate a Mindmap®, take a sheet of A3 paper and turn it horizontally (landscape format). Write the subject of the problem or the issue under consideration at the centre of the paper. Now follow these guidelines:

→ Starting from a central point, radiate out, drawing branches, graduating to sub-branches and then twigs
→ Use a different colour for each main branch
→ Write keywords in capitals – try to keep to one word per branch
→ If you have something negative to express, write the word down then cross it out
→ Be spontaneous
→ When finished, look for links, connections and ideas

Making links between different sub-subjects may lead to a breakthrough in solving the problem. On the page opposite is an example using our planned holiday again.

I find that I have expanded on some of the topics on the original list. For example, I want good weather but do not want to be too hot. Under 'Cost' I have included 'Friends', because we could share the cost of renting a villa or apartment. Considering Europe, I was stimulated to think of a beach, which then threw up an image of somewhere noisy and crowded; this

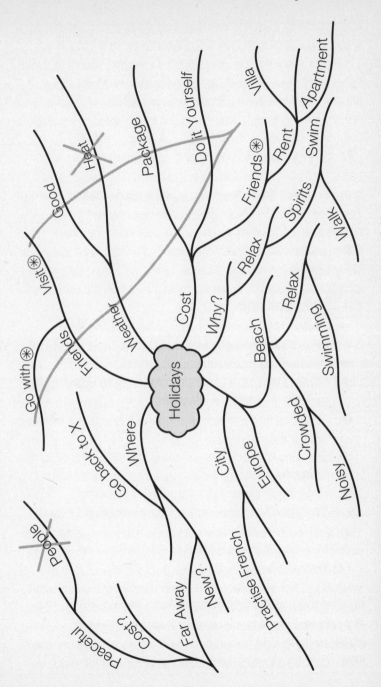

Using a Mindmap® to plan a holiday

made me think of what I wanted a holiday for in the first place, and the words 'Relax' and 'Sports' came into my mind.

It would seem that two themes have emerged: I want to avoid people and the subject of cost features several times. These seem to be my priorities. The original possibilities of practising French, visiting somewhere that might be crowded and going back to X have been abandoned.

I know what you are thinking: 'No one works with pen and paper these days; I do it all on my PC/laptop.' If this is your objection, there are software programs available, the best being *The Mind Manager*, which Tony Buzan was involved in developing. It uses colour and displays the flexibility inherent in the original pen-and-paper Mindmaps®. So there is no excuse!

 ## In practice

Some tasks lend themselves well to Mindmaps®:

→ Any planning or organising of activities.

→ Problem-solving, to allow you to arrive at a large number of different possible approaches.

→ Preparing presentations, particularly if looking for a fresh approach.

→ Clarifying what the problem *really* is before attempting the search for solutions.

→ Finding new possibilities. Lists are close-ended; Mindmaps® are open-ended – the branches may lead to new ideas.

→ Mindmaps® do not replace lists; rather they can be used in conjunction with lists.

Practise by choosing topics unconnected with your work. For example, imagine that you need to prepare a 15-minute presentation on your favourite hobby. Prepare a rough Mindmap®, then look at it critically and draw up a more

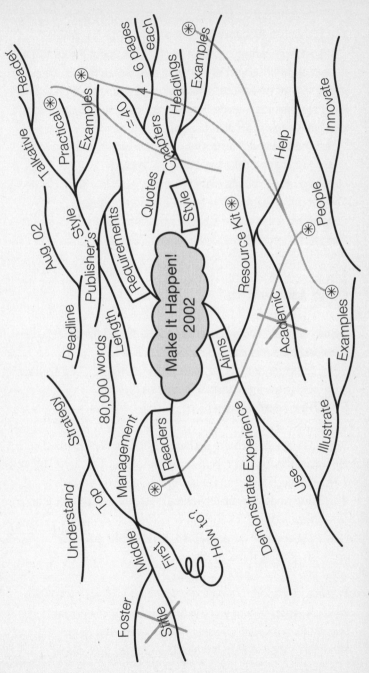

A Mindmap® for planning this book

structured map, eliminating some ideas, developing others and linking those that should be connected.

Alternatively, write a word or trigger concept in the centre and think of things associated with your concept. For example, 'shoe' throws up associations with sock, floor, polish, galoshes, rug, foot, staircase, ankle bracelet, dancing, etc. This exercise stimulates the associative powers of your mind.

So try a Mindmap® when you

→   are stuck for the solution to a problem
→   want to produce lots of ideas
→   want to explore the merits of different ideas
→   have little time to think along different lines
→   wonder what the problem *really* is

Case study

See the example on page 35 – this is the Mindmap® I have prepared for this book.

Further resources

Buzan, Tony, *The Mindmap Book*, BBC Books (1995).

O'Keeffe, John, *Mind Openers for Managers*, Thorsons (1994), in particular Chapter 4.

The Mind Manager software program, published by Mindjet.

Chapter 7
Fostering spontaneity – brainstorming

'It takes courage to be creative. As soon as you have an idea you are in a minority'
– E. PAUL TORRANCE, CREATIVITY RESEARCHER

'A new idea is delicate. It can be killed by a sneer or a yawn. It can be stabbed to death by a quip and worried to death by a frown on the right man's brow.'
– CHARLES BROWER

This American interactive technique is about 50 years old and is designed to enable a group to come up with as many ideas as possible on a given topic in a given time. Over the years, and perhaps as a result of crossing the Atlantic, the concept has become diluted. The idea of brainstorming now triggers mixed responses, but properly used it remains an immensely valuable tool.

The basic idea is to separate idea generation from idea evaluation, so as to create an environment free of criticism or judgement. People are asked to be spontaneous, so the spirit of a brainstorm is important. Try to create an atmosphere that allows people to relax, and keep proceedings light-hearted.

THE RULES

- Start with a warm-up
- Encourage wild ideas – any ideas
- Generate as many ideas as possible
- Build on other people's ideas
- Allow absolutely no evaluation, criticism or ridicule
- Aim for a group of between 5 and 10 people
- Have an enthusiastic leader
- Select a fast note-taker who does not filter ideas: allow positively no editing
- Restate the problem if the pace slackens
- Select a time limit of 20 to 30 minutes

→ **In practice**

→ Choose a non-intimidating room with windows.

→ For your warm-up, choose a completely irrelevant problem. For example, 'How many uses can we think of for a brick?' Give a three-minute time limit.

→ Write the ideas on a flip chart so all can see them.

→ Remove tables and chairs to encourage people to walk about. There is evidence that people think better and faster if they move.

→ Use incubation periods. Warn people of the problem to be brainstormed last thing one day. Then start the next day with the session. Unconsciously the brain will have made connections overnight.

→ Consider having the session after an informal buffet (not sit-down) lunch at which the problem may be discussed in a light-hearted way in a social setting.

→ Mix people from different departments to gather the maximum number of different standpoints.

→ Use volunteers, not conscripts.

➜ Discourage observers and people of widely different status: they tend to inhibit spontaneity.

Some situations are better for brainstorming than others, namely:

➜ Specific rather than general problems
➜ Problems that depend on idea-finding, not judgement
➜ Subjects in which imagination can play a part

Take great care how you define the topic for brainstorming. For example, 'How can we win new business?' is too general. Instead, break it down and devote a session to each specific issue:

➜ How can we attract new clients?
➜ How can we extend the commitment of our existing clients?
➜ How can we increase our market share from 16% to 19% by the end of next year?

➜ Try this

Suggest to your colleagues or team that a brainstorming session might be a way forward on some issue or problem. Having chosen the topic, volunteer to take part and organise the session yourself. Afterwards, read the notes carefully and reflect on the outcome.

In summary, brainstorming has the following advantages:

➜ It allows new ideas to survive the immediate judgement of peers
➜ It makes enthusiasm contagious
➜ It discourages inhibitions and defeatism
➜ It develops competitive spirit
➜ It is fun

Case studies

HOW NOT TO DO IT ...

I was once introducing German managers from a major IT group to techniques for generating ideas. When I mentioned brainstorming, people began to look embarrassed. I asked, 'Have you been involved in or conducted a brainstorming session?' After a short silence one manager said, 'Yes, and it doesn't work.' 'Oh,' I replied, 'tell me what happened.' He volunteered, 'Well, we tried. We got together, set a thirty-minute limit and nothing happened. No one said anything.' I asked, 'What problem or issue were you brainstorming?' A prolonged silence followed, with people looking at each other uneasily. 'Ah,' the manager said slowly, 'so you need a problem.'

This true story is a healthy reminder that nothing must be taken for granted.

HOW TO DO IT ...

This story concerns an oil company in Scandinavia. I was asked to conduct a two-day brainstorming session with the management board. We had a couple of meetings to identify the problem, which was eventually defined as 'How can we increase our market share from 10 per cent to 12 per cent in the next two years?'

On the first morning eight company representatives plus myself met in a small hotel. The issue was clearly written on a flip chart. After 30 minutes, with satisfactory results, we had a break, then I narrowed the issue down to 'How can we get more women into the petrol stations?' Many ideas flowed. We had another break, and then made the issue more general again: 'How can we attract more people into the petrol stations?' Other issues discussed that day were 'What should we improve to get repeat business and ensure customer loyalty?' and 'How can we differentiate our petrol stations from those of our competitors?' At the end of the first day all the ideas noted on flip charts were attached to the walls, sequentially.

On the second day we evaluated over 500 ideas. I used the PMI (Plus, Minus, Interesting) technique as a first screening process (see Chapter 8). We discussed the viability of every interesting idea in terms of current resources. Could it be developed and implemented? At the end of the second day half a dozen were selected for development.

Eighteen months later, ahead of schedule, the group had achieved their goal of a 2 per cent increase in market share.

Further resources

Evans, Peter, and Geoff Deehan, *The Keys to Creativity*, Grafton (1988), in particular pp. 138–47.

Kinsey Gorman, Carol, *Creative Thinking in Business*, Kogan Page (1989), in particular pp. 72–4.

Osborn, Alex, *Applied Imagination*, Scribner's, New York (1953). By the creator of brainstorming, an executive with Batten, Barton, Durstine & Osborn, Inc., one of the world's largest advertising agencies in the forties and fifties in the USA.

Chapter 8
Breaking the mould – lateral thinking

'The old thinking is not constructive enough. We need new thinking.'
– EDWARD DE BONO, PSYCHOLOGIST

'Walking along the road will not make you a better tennis player or a better skier.'
– EDWARD DE BONO

'Lateral thinking is a way of using information to escape from old ideas and to generate new ones.'
– EDWARD DE BONO

About 30 years ago Edward de Bono first coined the expression 'lateral thinking', which has since entered our everyday language. The technique consists of a series of tools to break existing thinking patterns and to view a situation from different standpoints.

Dr de Bono believes that we rely too much on logical thinking, which restricts our opportunities to think differently and challenge existing patterns. He has devised tools to help us change our attitudes, in particular to suspend judgement so as to give a new idea a chance of survival.

There are two levels of technique, using 'basic' or 'advanced' tools.

BASIC TOOLS

The basic tools are:

PMI (Plus, Minus, Interesting)
APC (Alternative Possible Choices) and
OPV (Other People's Views)

PLUS, MINUS, INTERESTING (PMI)

Consider the following statement: All cars should be bright yellow. Before giving a judgement, write down in three columns what would be good about this idea (Plus), what would be bad about the idea (Minus) and what could happen depending on other factors (Interesting). Limit yourself to a few minutes. You are probably finding that the most difficult column to fill in is the Interesting one. This is because we are used to thinking of new ideas in strictly positive or negative terms, and not to suspending judgement to consider shades of grey. The most valuable considerations are in the Interesting column because the outcome is still uncertain. Realising this, we begin to change our attitudes.

ALTERNATIVE POSSIBLE CHOICES (APC)

When faced with difficult situations, an APC evaluation can open up a productive stream of alternatives. For example, consider the following situation: Your manager keeps making unfair demands upon you. What are your possible courses of action? Your answer may explore the following options: ignore him or her, delegate up, escalate the situation, blackmail the manager, quit, ask for a transfer, ask for a meeting to clarify the situation, request help, and so on. APC can be used in situations where you are faced with decisions that seem to depend on conflicting alternatives. It helps you to explore the better choices, while keeping emotions at bay.

OTHER PEOPLE'S VIEWS (OPV)

How often have you been to a meeting, wishing to influence your boss, a colleague, a customer or a supplier, and failed?

It is often difficult to make other people see your point of view. To succeed you first need to see theirs, so that you can counteract with arguments that acknowlege their position. I will illustrate this with the example of a boss who does not delegate tasks to you. Your own arguments might be that you need the challenge, that you see your boss is overwhelmed, that you want to demonstrate your abilities, that you have not got enough to do, and so on. Now look at the situation from the point of view of your boss. It could be that he or she likes to be in control, thinks you are incompetent, does not like you, does not know how to delegate, and so on. If you can identify the right reason, you can adopt a strategy and arguments appropriate to the situation.

> ➜ **In practice**

- ➜ Use PMI as a way of approaching a new concept, suggestion or offer. It can be helpful in evaluating the results of a brainstorm.
- ➜ Use APC when faced with situations that seem to offer conflicting alternatives, to explore better choices.

➜   Use OPV to focus on specific people, to understand their
     motivation.

ADVANCED TOOLS

The advanced tools are:

REVERSAL

This is the simplest way of provoking the mind to think
differently. It can be expressed as turning an idea upside
down, standing it on its head, looking at it back to front,
and so on. It is a tool for changing a situation. Imagine, for
example, that a chairman has called a board meeting.
Imagine also that the board members are sceptical about
the value of another meeting. The situation could be
expressed in reverse as 'the board meeting has called the
chairman'. This reversal immediately changes the perception of the situation, suggesting that the board members
have something to say to the chairman, that the chairman
is an accessory to the meeting. The seat of power has
shifted. From a negative response, the board members
have switched to a positive attitude.

PO

To indicate to others and to ourselves that we are operating in a dynamic mode and not in a judgmental mode the
word 'po' (invented by Edward de Bono) is used. The
purpose of po is to stimulate the mind in an unexplored
area, to link unconnected ideas together. For example,
imagine that you wish to increase productivity in your
department. You choose a random object to consider
in association with your problem. Think, for example,
about the function of a curtain. Your situation can be

considered in terms of 'productivity in my department po curtain'.

ATTRIBUTES OF CURTAIN	POSSIBLE INNOVATIONS IN THE WORKPLACE
Hangs from one point	Remove all hierarchical levels
Moves freely from side to side	Institute a flexible work force, free to move between departments
Acts as a barrier	Improve communications
Open and shut once a day	Introduce 5-minute meetings at the beginning and end of each day

When using po, observe these rules:
- Use a concrete object that you can see
- Concentrate on the attributes of the object before you relate them to your problem.

 Try this

Find other people who have used lateral thinking. Form a club of interested people, starting with two or three others. Meet twice a month, formally but in a relaxed atmosphere, and practise.

For example, start with a PMI on the topic 'Everyone should wear a badge showing his or her mood'. Allow five minutes, and follow with a discussion on the value of undertaking a PMI, considering whether the strict time limit is a help or a constraint.

Over the months practise each tool in the same way. Keep a logbook. Avoid difficult questions when you practise, and maintain a spirit of fun. When all of you are at ease with the tools, try a work-related problem. If a member of the club lacks motivation, do not invite them back.

In my work I use all the tools above. Reversal is the most difficult to exploit successfully, but with all the others the results can be spectacular.

Further resources

All of Dr Edward de Bono's books, in particular *Serious Creativity*, HarperCollins (1992), *Lateral Thinking for Management*, Penguin (1971) and *Simplicity*, Penguin (1999).

Sherwood, Dennis, *Innovation Express*, Capstone (2002), in particular pp. 20–1 and 62–5.

Chapter 9
Transformations – understanding trends

'Trends are bottom-up, fads top-down.'
– JOHN NAISBITT, MANAGEMENT CONSULTANT AND
SOCIAL FORECASTER

'The power to become habituated to his surroundings is a
marked characteristic of mankind.'
– JOHN MAYNARD KEYNES, ECONOMIST

'When a change in perception takes place, the facts do
not change. Their meaning does.'
– PETER DRUCKER, MANAGEMENT CONSULTANT

A source of ideas lies in identifying, then understanding,
trends. Economic, demographic and sociological factors
mark transformations in our society that are taking place
right now as you read this book. If we are able to observe and
understand trends, we can become aware of opportunities.

TRENDS IN EVERYDAY LIFE

Consider how the electronic transfer of money has affected
banks. They have had to be innovative to respond to this
trend and devise ways of making their profits elsewhere.

Consider the issue of healthcare. In the past 30 years we have shifted from reliance on government to a culture of self-help. People have become interested in preventive measures through diets, exercise, and so on. They read about the issues – the proliferation of books on these subjects compared to 30 years ago is obvious – and they become more involved as they become more informed.

Consider leisure. Again, in the last 20 years people have shifted their interests. Nowadays we travel more; every town is equipped with a leisure centre and health clubs; there are more pubs competing with traditional restaurants and fast-food establishments.

Now if you were involved in any of these industries, would you have spotted the emerging patterns at the right time? Would you have seen the opportunities they offered?

 In practice

When an industry or a society is on the brink of a new order, entrepreneurs or politicians with vision and determination seize the moment. They take the world into the future. Ordinary mortals cling to their known past, unless pushed by such visionaries.

Examine some trends that may affect you.

FROM HIERARCHICAL STRUCTURES TO NETWORKING

If you have been working in a large organisation during the last 20 years you will have witnessed a shift from pyramidal structures to teams, to matrix systems of reporting, and to the encouragement of networking.

A network is a loose group of people who share ideas, information and perhaps resources. With the help of technology they communicate electronically, as well as on the phone, at parties, and so on. The impact of networking on working practice is considerable.

As an employee, you need to use the right tactics to get noticed. If you are in middle management, you have the opportunity to introduce new working practices if appropriate.

As hierarchies shrink, you need to consider your colleagues on a more equal basis if you are a senior manager. This may affect the way you run your meetings, for example. As people are encouraged to network inside and outside your organisation, new ideas will be introduced. This will increase communication and may encourage experimentation.

As more people network, more flexibility will be introduced into the workforce. People will come and go more freely; age groups will be less static; pension arrangements may change. Human resources departments will adapt their recruitment procedures and remuneration packages accordingly.

FROM UNIVERSITY TO HOME LEARNING

Another trend touches on three factors: electronics, the commitment of European governments to creating more graduates, and the cost of maintaining university buildings.

As more students are admitted to higher education, this creates pressure on teaching facilities and accommodation. One London college recently had to pay £20 million to comply with Health and Safety regulations for just one building. But with increasing access to the Internet, a student can now download the necessary learning materials in his or her own room. Would it not make sense to use technology more, for the student to work predominantly at home, perhaps going into university just one week each term for experiments and tutorials, thus saving a lot of taxpayers' money?

REAPING THE BENEFITS

Recognising trends enables managers to position their organisation to take advantage of transformations in society.

Case study

A major international company formed a unit to consider possible future scenarios in order to help it plan its activities. It was deemed not enough simply to consider what would happen if the price of an essential service or product went up or down or if some new law or tax came into effect. To plan future actions and keep their options open, managers responsible for formulating company strategy were asked much more open questions:

→ What two questions would you most want to ask an oracle?

→ What is a good scenario?

→ What is a bad scenario?

→ If you could go back as far as you are looking ahead now, what would then have been a useful scenario?

→ What are the most important decisions you face right now?

→ What constraints do you feel the company's culture puts upon you in making these decisions?

→ What do you want on your epitaph?

The issues were discussed within groups of managers. All sorts of hidden questions, agendas and ideas came out into the open. These were freely discussed between colleagues who would never have done so in the normal course of their work.

Three criteria were maintained throughout the discussions:

→ To build the various scenarios it was crucial that they should be in line with company *strategic* vision.

→ The *competitive position* of the company was assessed against managers' perceptions of customers and competitors' views of the company.

→ It was most important to keep *options open* for future proactive or reactive adjustments to situations that might develop in the future. This ran against the normal preference of managers for following their own pet ideas, which usually did not entertain other options.

This method of planning led the company to:

→ Seize opportunities that arose unexpectedly in the future and

→ Avoid the worst effects of a downturn when the industry was hit.

Further resources

Naisbitt, John, *Megatrends*, Futura (1982).

Schwarz, Peter, *The Art of the Long View*, Doubleday (1992).

Senge, Peter, et al., *The Fifth Discipline Fieldbook*, Nicholas Brealey (1994), Chapter 41.

Timperley, John, *Network Your Way to Success*, Piatkus (2002).

Chapter 10
Input/output – mapping sources of opportunity

'The guiding principle in our efforts is to identify the value
added – and cut out the rest.'
– MICHAEL BALLÉ, PROFESSOR OF MANAGEMENT

'The basic tool for diagnosing competitive advantage and
finding ways to enhance it is the value chain, which
divides a firm into the discrete activities it performs in
designing, producing, marketing and distributing its
product.'
– MICHAEL PORTER, MANAGEMENT THEORIST AND
HARVARD PROFESSOR

Business process re-engineering aims to provide a method
for improving processes in practice, with the least disrup-
tion to work-in-hand and the fastest operational results. It
is an inward-looking process that requires you to examine
rigorously the flow of activities your organisation or
department performs from product design or conception
to its implementation in the marketplace, comprising
purchasing, production, service, and so on.

Improving your process systems is based on the belief
that there must be a better way of doing what we do; it is

similar to the Japanese *kaizen* principle of continuous improvement. Opportunities for innovation based on process systems can be found in abundance if you apply a systematic approach.

In his book *Competitive Advantage* Michael Porter offers an excellent tool for performing this examination. He divides the activities of a typical organisation into five areas, as shown in the diagram below.

The first three activities, **Input**, **Operations** and **Output**, are logical and self-explanatory. Something comes in

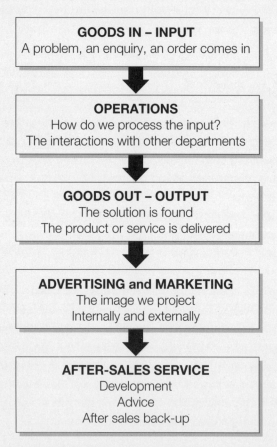

GOODS IN – INPUT
A problem, an enquiry, an order comes in

OPERATIONS
How do we process the input?
The interactions with other departments

GOODS OUT – OUTPUT
The solution is found
The product or service is delivered

ADVERTISING and MARKETING
The image we project
Internally and externally

AFTER-SALES SERVICE
Development
Advice
After sales back-up

Sources of opportunity in your organisation

(a problem, an order, raw materials) and forms the Input into the organisation. Operations represent how we deal with the Input. Output covers the solution to the problem, the delivery to the customer, the product made from raw materials.

Two other areas, **Image** and **After-Sales**, are different. Image relates to the way we are perceived by customers, other departments, the media, competitors and suppliers. After-Sales considers what your department does once it has delivered the product or service to the customer.

Finding ways to improve processes in these five areas of your organisation leads to competitive advantage.

 In practice

If you wish to improve your process systems, get your team together for a day and present them with copies of the diagram. You may find it useful to opt for a brainstorming session, based on a question focused on improvement. For example, for Input ask: 'How could we improve the way we receive enquiries?', or 'How do we welcome customers better?', or 'In what way could we improve the delivery of our raw materials?'

In terms of Image, you could ask: 'How are we perceived by customers?', 'How could we project a better image?', 'What could we do to make outsiders see we are the best at X?'

After collecting dozens of ideas for improving performance in each area (Input, Operations, Output, Image and After-Sales), ask your team to select two ideas for each area which would make the most impact upon your performance or deliver better customer value. Ask for volunteers to implement these changes and set a deadline for when these improvements will be completed. Review as a team the progress you make.

A FINAL THOUGHT

Discovering sources of opportunity requires involvement with, and understanding of, the outside world. An understanding of the competition and customers leads to rapid results, but it requires a continuous effort. You will need such an understanding to improve your process systems, and in developing it you will uncover strong and weak points in these systems, which can then be maximised or remedied as necessary.

Further resources

Ballé, Michael, *The Business Process Re-engineering Action Kit*, Kogan Page (1995), in particular Chapters 1, 4 and 10.
Hammer, Michael, and J. Champy, *Re-engineering the Corporation*, HarperCollins (1993).
Porter, Michael, *Competitive Advantage*, Free Press (1985), in particular the Preface and Chapters 1, 2 and 13.

Chapter 11

The outside world – creating new markets

'Successful entrepreneurs do not wait until the "Muse kisses them" and gives them a "bright idea"; they go to work.'
– PETER DRUCKER, MANAGEMENT CONSULTANT

You have already tried, I am sure, ways to improve what you do *within* your organisation. But have you given thought and effort to what happens *outside* it? Successful innovators exploit the changes they have perceived in the 'outside world' to create new markets.

Consider the success of the upmarket sandwich chain Pret à Manger on both sides of the Atlantic.

Sinclair Beecham, the British co-founder of the firm, understood early in 2000 that, on Wall Street, lunch is for wimps. Staying in with a sandwich is dedication to duty. Quite a culture change from the excesses of the 1980s. Combining this insight with their expertise, Pret combines the new-found sandwich-at-the-desk ethos of New Yorkers with the exoticism they like: Sushi in a box.
(SUNDAY TIMES, 4 FEBRUARY 2001)

To help you identify market opportunities, focus on five factors:
- Customers
- Competition
- Changes in the industry
- Environment
- New knowledge

By systematically and regularly paying attention to these five factors you will optimise your chances of developing new market opportunities. Here is how:

 Try this

CUSTOMERS

A definition I like is 'A customer is a relationship'. Treat your customer as a close friend. Imagine for a minute that you have not heard from a friend in a while. Would you send a third party to see how she is? No, you would pick up the phone, or send an e-mail, yourself. The same should apply to your customers. Go and see them, and with each one discuss the following:

→ What are their key problems and concerns?

→ What are their key requirements?

→ Do your current products or services make a major improvement to their performance?

→ What does your product or service cost them beyond what you charge them?

→ What new products or services would result in a significant improvement in their service?

Notice that I am not suggesting market research. The aim of your dialogue is for the customer to grasp that you are an ally. You can help; you are prepared to listen. In exchange, you must be ready to question the quality of your product or service. Accept criticism. This will lead to your developing new ideas to meet customer needs.

COMPETITION

Similarly, try to get an understanding of competitors' products or services through customers' eyes. Together, consider:

→ Why do some customers go to the competition?
→ What added value does a competitor bring to a customer?
→ Are there markets not addressed by competitors?
→ Could we address these markets ourselves?

CHANGES IN THE INDUSTRY

Here is an exercise for you and your team. Jot down all the changes you have observed in your industry in the last five years. You could start by considering whether there has been a shift in your organisation from traditional employees to contract staff. Has your HR department learnt how to manage these people productively? My personal list would look like this:

→ e-mail has replaced fax
→ 50% of business is generated by my associates (it used to be less than 10%)
→ People approach me to work with me
→ Changes in presentation styles: Powerpoint, etc.
→ I use a laptop and a mobile for work now
→ Universities are now an important part of business
→ More work in Europe
→ The growing demand for coaching executives

As you compile your list, ask yourself and other people: Is there an emerging industry or service that we have ignored? As markets change, shrink or grow, can we adapt what we do to newly defined or emerging needs?

ENVIRONMENT

This is a good subject for an 'away-day'. Get your team to reflect on changing environmental factors, for example the changes in demographics. By 2030, 50 per cent of Britons will be aged over 50 yet with large disposable incomes. If you are in the leisure industry, this could be significant. Think about the emergence of e-commerce (supermarket shopping and delivery): if you are in the retail or packaging industries this may be interesting. Examine emerging trends in our social, economic, political, technological and perceptual environment. Then select a couple and get your group to work out how you can adapt your products or service to meet this newly identified need.

NEW KNOWLEDGE

Human knowledge is continually increasing. Not a day goes by without new ideas, thoughts, inventions and discoveries. These are widely reported in daily newspapers and specialist periodicals. When you read about them, think of your business. How could this affect me? For example, we are now beginning to understand how memory works. Would this affect your business if you were in the publishing world? Similarly, we know that British people have grown just over an inch in height on average in the last 100 years. If you were a car or aeroplane designer, how would this influence your products?

POINTS TO NOTE

What is important throughout this exercise is to raise the right questions, be it with your customers or your team. Here are some tips:

- Keep a record of their answers
- Revisit your records, say every six months

- Assign responsibility to a member of your team for detecting, monitoring and analysing trends
- Use your relationship with a trusted customer to explore possibilities in terms of the five factors discussed above

Case study

Early in 2000 a tyre service company needed to reassess the service it gave to its truck fleet customers. The reasons for the reassessment were simple and twofold: to enable the company to keep ahead of its competitors, and to increase market share.

The culture in the company had hitherto been to sell as many tyres as possible. The policy for achieving this was to slash prices and offer the customer cheaper brands. This tactic led one customer to exclaim, 'The more you slash the tyre price, the more the total bill increases.'

The management embarked on a significant dialogue with the firm's existing customers, posing the questions 'What are your key concerns? What are your key requirements? What new service would result in a significant improvement in your performance?' The last question, in particular, revealed that having the trucks on the road – i.e. off the road for the minimum time possible – was the commonest and most pressing concern for fleet operators.

The management team consolidated the data collected and implemented improvements to their service by entering into three- to five-year agreements with customers (rather than one year, as before), enabling them to get the best out of their tyres. From being a product provider the company switched its culture to that of a service provider with the commercial tools to support it. For example, tyres were regrooved rather than replaced indiscriminately, and the customer obtained more miles per tyre; at regular intervals tread depth was measured, pressures checked, and a general fleet inspection conducted. A single invoicing procedure was also introduced. Customers benefited enormously from these preventive and diagnostic actions – there were fewer breakdowns on the road and, as a result, the trucks were now more on the road than off.

Similarly, the tyre service company has benefited by a substantially increased market share, its image in the business has been boosted, and so has its profitability. This new culture has led to a reorganisation of its fitting units. But that's another story!

Further resources

Drucker, Peter, *Innovation and Entrepreneurship*, Harper & Row (1985), in particular Chapters 1, 6, 7, 8 and 9.

Drucker, Peter, 'They're Not Employees, They're People', *Harvard Business Review* (February 2002).

MacMilland, Ian C., and Rita Gunther McGrath, 'Discovering New Points of Differentiation', *Harvard Business Review on Innovation*, Harvard Business School Publishing Corporation (2001), p. 131.

Sherwood, Dennis, *Innovation Express*, Capstone (2002), in particular Chapter 6.

Thomke, Stefan, and Eric von Hippel, 'Customers as Innovators: New Ways to Create Value', *Harvard Business Review* (April 2002).

Ulwick, Anthony W., 'Turn Customer Input into Innovation', *Harvard Business Review* (January 2002).

Chapter 12
Screening ideas – the matrix method

'An idea isn't worth much until a man is found who has the energy and ability to make it work.'
– WILLIAM FEATHER, WRITER AND PUBLISHER

The matrix method is a process for an initial screening of ideas that makes the facts visible and does not give undue weight to excessive quantification too soon. Although it has the weakness of no customer focus, it will help you to prioritise ideas, take resources into account during evaluations, and apply criteria for the selection of ideas.

You need to have a broad focus during the screening stage. An evaluation that is purely financial or people oriented, for example, is not likely to be successful. Financially oriented selections tend to be too constraining, while people-oriented evaluations lack focus. Ideally, screening should fulfil a number of objectives.

HOW TO USE THE MATRIX

The matrix below shows two axes: one deals with the question of strategic fit and benefits to the department; the other addresses the question of ease and cost of implementation. When you evaluate a new idea, the aim is to find the perfect match between the two. Start with the vertical axis.

Strategic Fit and Benefit questions whether the idea is in line with your strategy and business objectives. Does it tie in with the nature and direction of your business? What will the benefits be in terms of productivity, market share, the quality of your service or product and your profitability?

If the answers to these are definitely 'Good' on a scale of 'Good, OK, Bad', go to the top line of the matrix.

Ease and Cost of Implementation measures the idea against four resources: People, Time, Systems and the overall Cost.

- **People**: Do we have enough skilled resources? Who will it affect? Will we meet resistance?
- **Time**: How long will it take to develop and implement this idea?
- **Systems**: Do we need to change our systems and procedures? Do we have the technology?
- **Cost**: What will it cost to market and promote this idea? In particular with regard to people (will we need to retrain or recruit more?) and systems (will we need to upgrade our technology?)

If the answers to these questions are definitely 'Good', go to the right-hand side of the matrix, as shown opposite.

Best is applicable if you have a close strategic fit, high benefits, easy implementation and low costs. Go for it.

Highly Probable results from good strategic benefit and reasonable costs or reasonable strategic benefit and low costs. Try to improve the weaker factor.

Possible means that both strategic benefit and implementation costs could do with improvement. Work on the idea.

	Bad	OK	Good
Good	Possible	Highly Probable	**BEST**
OK	Remote	Possible	Highly Probable
Bad	No	No	No

Strategic Fit and Benefit (row labels, left side)

Ease and Cost of Implementation

Ease and cost of implementation versus strategic fit and benefit

Remote indicates that both strategic fit and costs are poor. Not a good idea.

No. Forget the idea.

 Try this

You need to be clear about your strategy or business objectives. Involve two other close colleagues or team members for an objective evaluation.

Put all the ideas to be considered to the matrix test. Then rank the ideas from 'Best' through to 'No'. This gives you the priority to work on. Priority for ideas that rank equally may be refined using the 'Three Rs' or 'Does It Fit?' tests (see Chapter 14).

When there is disagreement about the positioning of an idea, seek other opinions.

Further resources

Michalko, Michael, *Thinkertoys*, Ten Speed Press (1991), in particular the last chapter, 'Endtoys'.

Chapter 13
Cultivating dialogue – how to listen

'One friend, one person who is truly understanding, who takes the trouble to listen to us as we consider our problem, can change our whole outlook on the world.'
– DR ELTON MAYO, WRITER AND INDUSTRIAL PSYCHOLOGIST

Research shows that we spend 46 per cent of our waking time listening, 30 per cent speaking, 16 per cent reading and 8 per cent writing. And yet, were you taught to listen?

In innovation, listening plays an important part. Many books and articles exhort the would-be innovator to listen to customers. This, they say, is one of the most reliable sources of ideas. Yes, but how do you do it?

UNDERSTAND YOUR CUSTOMERS

There are dangers inherent in asking customers what they want, in that we may simply get a wish list. The problem with wish lists is that the items suggested may be expensive to produce and not every customer will want to buy them. The cost of responding to every customer's needs is prohibitive. Instead, concentrate on the desired outcomes behind the wish list. These are values that will be shared by many customers.

Take an ice-cream maker. If asked, many people will say, 'I want an ice-cream maker that I can just use and put in the freezer when I have a surplus of fruit.' A surplus of fruit is something one notices when it is almost too late: if not dealt with soon, the fruit will rot and be wasted. So speed, ease of operation and little or no aftercare are what the user needs but rarely asks for. Thus a machine that needs no cooling time, is easy to assemble, with a large capacity, and which can then be forgotten in the freezer is what the user is really looking for. And yet go to a department store and the number of ice-cream makers combining these qualities is negligible.

So listen to customers, yes, but do not stop there. Enter into a dialogue and challenge what you hear. Customers are poor at imagining what they don't know about. Their terms of reference are limited. This is where your intuition, knowledge and expertise can dovetail with their wish list. You can see and expand possibilities beyond what you hear.

 Try this

Select a group of customers with whom you already have a good relationship. Ask what else you could provide for them. For each suggestion, ask why.

Prepare a series of targeted open-ended questions. For example: What would my innovation bring to them? What would they save? What is the attraction for their customers? What is the attraction for their suppliers?

Look for a pattern in the responses. If there is a pattern, consider its implications. What ideas are there here for you? How can you adapt your business practices so as to respond to your customers' needs?

In practice

If your main source of innovation is your existing customers, you will need to formalise your interactions with them. Pay attention to:

→ Finding those who have a strong need to renew their own products or services quickly.

→ Those who have staff with experience and can help you if you get stuck.

→ Keeping a note of your customers' ideas – what is not useful today may be resuscitated tomorrow.

→ How large, or small, your customer is. Some are very sophisticated and need cutting-edge approaches. Many will not understand, or be ready for, a revolutionary idea. You should know which are which.

Further resources

Steil, Lyman K., Joanne Summerfield and George de Mare, *Listening – It Can Change Your Life*, McGraw-Hill (1983).

Sutton, Robert I., 'The Weird Rules of Creativity', *Harvard Business Review* (September 2001).

Ulwick, Anthony W., 'Turn Customer Input into Innovation', *Harvard Business Review* (January 2002).

Chapter 14
Narrowing the field – choosing an idea

*'It's just as sure a recipe for failure to have the right idea
fifty years too soon as fifty years too late.'*
– J. R. PLATT, WRITER AND SCIENTIST

Once you have generated and screened ideas, you need to
select one (or perhaps more, but not too many at any one
time) to develop. Your success as an innovator depends on
it. In this chapter you will find two reliable techniques.

THE THREE RS

Popularised in the 1980s by Kenichi Ohmae of McKinsey
& Co., this requires the idea to be judged simultaneously
in terms of **Reality, Ripeness** and **Resources**.

Reality means that the idea should take account of the
customer and his wishes, the competition and the
company's field of competence.

Ripeness means timing. Will the marketplace be ready
for and receptive to the idea?

Resources are required to develop and market the idea.
Does the organisation have them?

Each idea is submitted to close scrutiny under these three headings.

 Try this

If you have an idea you wish to pursue, put it through the Three Rs test.

→ First, **Reality**. Do customers want it? Do you have first-hand knowledge of this? Could it be copied easily by competitors?

→ Second, **Ripeness**. Are people's attitudes in the market-place at large open to this idea? Is it too late or too early?

→ Finally, **Resources**. Do you have the expertise to carry it through? Can you obtain financial backing? Do you have the technology needed?

Do this on your own if you have a tempting idea, or apply the test with your team when you evaluate the results of a brainstorm.

A WORD OF CAUTION

Applying the Three Rs does not guarantee success: any new idea carries an element of risk. The gamble of making the final choice is the narrow gate the innovator has to pass through.

This warning applies also to our next technique.

DOES IT FIT?

This is a structured approach to selecting an idea before embarking on its development. It is inspired by Gifford Pinchot III, intrapreneur and consultant, who says that a good idea simultaneously fulfils three different needs:

• Organisational Needs
• Innovative Team Needs
• Customers' Needs

Does It Fit? has two stages. Apply the initial evaluation before you develop your idea. It is a simple but rigorous method to be used before you involve your manager.

FIRST STAGE

Scrutinise your idea against these questions:

1. Organisational Needs
It is utopian to think that your ideas always match what your management wants.
- Do you know your organisational or departmental goals? Does the idea fit?
- Does it fit the culture of your organisation?

2. Innovative Team Needs
The difference between creative people and innovators is that innovators are determined that their idea will succeed. They are ready to foster and defend it and strive towards successful implementation.
- Does this idea fit the kind of person you are? Does it respect your values? Is it the sort of thing you like doing?
- If you get stuck, do you know experts who can join the team to help you?

3. Customers' Needs
Unless you have a market, the idea will not take off.
- Has a customer asked for this? Can you interest others?
- Does it meet a need?

If you reply 'No' to any of the above, see whether you can modify your idea. If you can't, drop it.

If you reply 'Yes', you will need to persuade your

manager and/or the management team. It is now time to ask yourself and your team deeper questions.

SECOND STAGE

1. Organisational Needs
- Will this idea give your organisation a unique advantage? Is it in timing or market position, or is the idea something that could be patented?
- Are there risks? Can you identify them? Can you see how to overcome them?
- Do you know what people are prepared to pay? How will this translate into profits and margins?

2. Innovative Team Needs
- Does the team have a good spread of skills?
- Do you have some experience in this field?
- Can you think of a high-level sponsor?

3. Customers' Needs
- Is your product or service significantly better than that offered by the competition? In what way?
- Does it help your customer save money or time?
- Can you think of a pricing strategy?
- What value or benefit will it bring to the customer?

When you have positive answers to the above questions you are in a strong position to talk to your management and the financial department to negotiate for a budget.

 In practice

Apply the first set of questions, as shown below. Modify the idea as necessary to eliminate flaws.

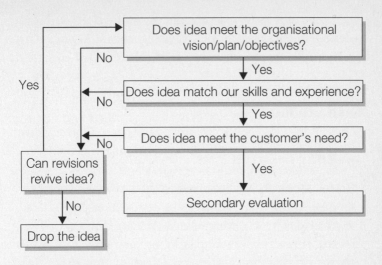

Does it fit? First-stage questions

If the idea still has potential, apply the second checklist (below). This will provide you with the arguments to convince management of the validity of the idea.

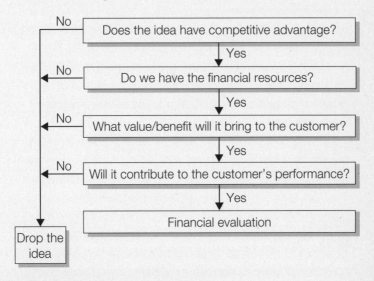

Does it fit? Second-stage questions

It may be necessary, depending on the magnitude and potential impact of your idea, to write a business plan. The questions above can serve as a framework.

Case studies

FAILING THE THREE RS

Coca-Cola lost their sense of reality when, in the early 1980s, they replaced their old recipe with a new 'improved' one. This was not what the customer wanted. At great cost they had to retrieve product made according to the new recipe in order to reinstate the old. Market share consequently suffered.

In the 1970s the garbage disposal unit for kitchen sinks flopped on the Japanese market. At that time the sewage systems in Japan's major cities were not capable of handling the additional load. The idea and the time were not ripe.

EMI, a British firm, developed and launched the world's first X-ray computerised tomography (CT) scanner. However, the company lacked the human resources to market the product aggressively and the financial resources for additional R&D. Soon GE, Siemens and Philips, who had strong marketing and R&D resources, extended the original CT concept to other beams and rays, including ultrasonic and nuclear magnetic resonance scans.

MAKING SURE IT FITS

The Toyota Motor Company production system, known as Just In Time, has revolutionised manufacturing. Taiichi Ohno, its inventor, thought it unnecessary to stockpile large quantities of components for production assembly lines. The company introduced a computer system whereby component suppliers are sent a production plan. This is followed by a reminder so the supplier can meet the assembly line schedule. The supplier delivers components to the conveyor belt just as they are needed during assembly.

The same Mr Ohno of Toyota also understood that every customer wants a personalised car. To meet customers' demands, dealers collect the information regarding customers' required specifications and pass the order to the factory. Here 'signposts' in the main assembly line indicate the model, type and specifications of each car, and all the components of that particular vehicle are assembled there and then, using the Just In Time procedures.

Taiichi Ohno is clearly an innovator with the vision and determination needed to make innovation happen. He thought of new systems that saved his company money and distanced them from the competition. He also met customer needs: the car people want is delivered in less than half the time it used to take.

Further resources

Ohmae, Kenichi, *The Mind of the Strategist*, Penguin (1982), in particular Chapters 5 and 7.

Pinchot, Gifford, III, *Intrapreneuring*, Harper & Row (1985), in particular Chapters 5 and 6.

Chapter 15
Conveying the message – presenting your idea

'Having the idea is easy. Getting the guts to go out and do it is the hard part.'
– DEAN BUTLER, FOUNDER OF VISION EXPRESS

At some stage you will have to turn your idea into reality. This means mastering two skills: converting your intuition into a business plan, and presenting it with confidence. I have seen more ideas fail at this stage than at any other. Innovators are not good at sequential thinking early on. They prefer experimentation to a rigid plan. Unfortunately, many managers prefer detailed plans over loose ends. Can we bridge the gap?

Have you ever presented a new idea with flawless logic, impeccable data and the passion of a preacher, only to be told that it can't be done, the timing is wrong, or every project has been frozen; or worse, 'I can't see what's in it for us.' Why? you wonder. Perhaps it is because you do not know how to adapt your presentation to decision-makers.

In this chapter we will look at writing a business plan and how to tailor your presentation to the decision-maker confronting you.

PLANNING YOUR BUSINESS PLAN

The purpose of a business plan is threefold:
- to enable you to get yourself organised
- to interest your management
- to convince decision-makers to give you permission to proceed

→ Try this

→ Start by writing an *executive summary* on one sheet of A4. This overview must demonstrate without any doubt why your company needs to embrace your idea.

→ Next, explain how your idea *fits* your organisation's direction, why customers would want it, and how existing resources will suffice – at least at the beginning.

→ Give a *timetable* with progress milestones.

→ Include a paragraph on *risks*; this could include the risk of not going ahead, the risk from the competition, and the measured risk that is inherent in any innovation.

→ Add a *marketing plan*. Show possible expansion of the idea, how it could be rolled on.

THE ART OF PRESENTING

Too often, when people are preparing to convey their ideas to someone else, particularly their boss, they focus on themselves: their style, their message. This is a mistake. Effective presenters tailor the message to the individual facing them. So do not start by seeing things *your* way; instead begin by seeing things *their* way.

Try this

KNOW YOUR BOSS!

If your boss is new, research how she or he makes decisions. If you have been together for some time, reflect on the following points:

→ Some people like to have lots of data and be given the time to digest it

→ Others prefer to know that another executive is already in favour of your proposal

→ Some are receptive to a well-structured, flawless case

→ A few act quickly if the idea sounds simple, is easily grasped and seems like fun

LIMIT YOUR INFORMATION

Why do you want to say so much? Flooding your boss with information will detract from your message. Research shows that after 20 minutes people's concentration decreases. If your boss likes lots of data, wait until she or he asks for it.

SMILE – IT'S INFECTIOUS

If you are not enthusiastic about your idea, who will be? If you are not relaxed with it, your boss will be nervous and will delay the decision.

CONNECT

Involve your boss. Engage him or her in a discussion. Invite questions.

In practice

When you are ready, *write your business plan*. Pay great attention to the executive summary, which can make or break your venture. Make it objective. Explain clearly what your idea is, show the benefit to your company and your clients, and make clear your commitment to it. Summarise the timetable and marketing plan. Your management needs to be convinced that you have thought it through.

Show the plan to colleagues and listen to their comments.

Prepare your *presentation*. Rehearse with colleagues or team members who know your boss, get them to play him or her. Adapt your presentation in the light of their feedback.

Case study

This concerns a blue-chip company in IT. I had been involved with them for several years, helping to make their managers in Europe more aware of how crucial their roles in fostering innovation were. One day I was asked by one of their directors to coach an English manager. This person – we will call him Frank – had an idea. He had found a way of taking the company's technology to schools in the UK and the rest of Europe. The company was very keen to do this at minimum cost but with maximum exposure. Frank had found a way.

Frank's career had been in marketing, primarily in Europe. He had lots of contacts, a large network. He was 58 and did not fit the stereotype of the marketing person. Modest and a good listener, he was quiet, organised and exuded solidity. I asked him to present his idea to me.

At first I could not follow him. He avoided my eyes, scribbled obscure graphs on a flip chart, embarked on a monologue which I did not understand, and then stopped. That was his presentation. I asked him to work on it. Could he prepare the graphs in advance and draft a written presentation that summed up in succinct terms the benefits to his firm and to the schools?

A couple of weeks later we met again. This time he was a lot clearer and I followed the approach. The technical problem had been identified and solved. But I was still worried by Frank's lack of openness. He still avoided my eyes. So I tackled this. 'How can I put my trust in you if you seem unsure of yourself? There is something else here, Frank, that I am not grasping.' After a short silence he confided at last: 'Well, I am fifty-eight and could retire at sixty. If I get the green light for this project, it is a commitment for three years, perhaps more. I am not sure I want to do this. I am not sure what my family thinks.'

So we uncovered the real issue from Frank's point of view. There was a personal problem in addition to the technical one – the lack of a personal commitment to the idea on his part. We discussed the pros and cons of retirement and agreed that he had to resolve it by the time we next met.

He decided, after talking it over with his family, that he would stay on and, if allowed, take the project all over Europe. Accordingly, the personal problem was solved. He made his presentation to the board and it was approved.

I met him four years later, a happy man. He was about to retire. The project had been successfully implemented. He was leaving with a better pension, and his name was known throughout Europe, linked with a unique project.

There cannot be clarity of thought unless there is commitment of the heart.

Further resources

Pinchot, Gifford, III, *Intrapreneuring*, Harper & Row (1985), in particular the Appendix.

Timperley, John, *Network Your Way to Success*, Piatkus (2002), in particular Chapter 8.

Williams, Gary A., and Robert B. Miller, 'Change the Way You Persuade', *Harvard Business Review* (May 2002).

Part 2:
Development – turning
an idea into a reality

Chapter 16
Defining your strategy – the six-point plan

'Companies need two systems. One to run the business and one to develop new ideas.'
– ANDRALL E. PEARSON, FORMER PRESIDENT OF PEPSICO

'Innovation is work ... In innovation as in any other work there is talent, there is ingenuity, there is predisposition. But when all is said and done, innovation becomes hard, focused, purposeful work making very great demand on diligence, on persistence, and on commitment. If these are lacking, no amount of talent, ingenuity or knowledge will avail.'
– PETER DRUCKER, MANAGEMENT CONSULTANT, FROM *INNOVATION AND ENTREPRENEURSHIP*

Have a look in your wardrobe. Can you spot any garments fastened with Velcro? Glance around your sitting room. Are your curtains secured with it? Recall your last haircut. Was not your gown kept together at the top with ... yes, you've guessed, Velcro tape! But do you know how it was invented? Here is the story.

THE STORY OF VELCRO

In 1948 George de Mestral returned from a hunting trip in the Swiss mountains annoyed by the burrs that clung to his clothing and the hairs of his dog. He was puzzled. What made them stick? He discovered that it was the combination of the loops in the weave of his clothing and the hooks on the burrs. Having trained as an engineer, de Mestral suddenly had an idea. What if he could cover strips of cloth with tiny hooks that would cling like burrs? Could he make a synthetic version?

Eight years passed, marked by disappointments and false starts. De Mestral had gone to textile experts in Lyons; their initial efforts were laborious and costly. He asked some Swiss colleagues to design a loom capable of producing tapes of loops and hooks in quantity; they failed. On his own, de Mestral finally constructed a new loom and, using infrared technology (which helps the glue set) and a new adhesive invented by Du Pont, at last he produced quantities of tapes containing loops. It was 1956. He still had to produce hooks.

One day the solution came to him. He stopped at a barber's shop, bought a pair of clippers and snipped each loop, which took a very long time. Simultaneously, an American became interested and at last adapted the process to the loom. By 1959 Velcro had become a commercial success. Today Velcro Industries NV systematically looks for incremental improvements in the tape and new consumer applications in, among others, the medical, aircraft and clothing industries.

I use the Velcro story to illustrate the Six-Point Plan. This is a *systematic* approach to planning the development of an idea.

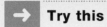 **Try this**

1 WHAT IS YOUR TARGET AREA?

The goal, target area or objective of your innovation must be clear in your mind and your team's. *(De Mestral wanted to reproduce the hooks he had observed in nature and the loops to be found in textile weaves.)*

A customer should help define the goal whenever possible. *(In Part 1, Ideas, most techniques emphasise the need to involve the customer.)*

If necessary, analyse the market segment you are aiming at, your target customers, the size of the market, the specific nature of the service and its benefits for users. How will competitors enter the market, and how may entry be made difficult for them? *(Velcro Industries puts a lot of effort into exploring new customer applications.)*

2 DEFINE YOUR STRATEGY

To reach your goal you need a plan. This has to show *what* you hope to accomplish, by *when*. It may include a marketing and sales plan, a summary of the risks and costs involved, and the benefits to be expected.

Actions must be arranged in order of priority. *(At the start of his venture, in 1948, de Mestral went to see his banker – a friend of his – who agreed to advance finance until 1955; but first he needed a business plan.)*

3 WHAT RESOURCES DO YOU NEED?

For your idea to succeed you need at least the following resources (more specific ones will emerge from the analysis above):

1. The support of management: do you have a sponsor?
2. Finance.
3. Time: defined in a schedule indicating when various activities will take place.
4. People: you may have to consider bringing into your project other people who have special expertise. They may include your customer. *(Some organisations, such as 3M, allow staff a specific period of time to work on any project they like. This gives employee and employer the flexibility to experiment without an official accounting of resources. When that time has passed, and if the idea looks promising, specific resources are allocated. De Mestral had a fair idea of the resources he needed and he went to the experts.)*

4 WHERE WOULD YOU LIKE TO BE BY SPECIFIC TIMES?

Your timetable or schedule of activities should detail milestones. What target will you have reached, and by when? *(If there was a flaw in de Mestral's plan, this was it: he had no specific deadline.)*

5 WHAT OBSTACLES MIGHT YOU ENCOUNTER?

Consider now the problems your project may encounter during its development. These may include competition, a negative response from some customers, loss of management enthusiasm, loss of resources, a general business turndown, or a new risk assessment. *(De Mestral knew the obstacles he faced: those inherent in designing a loom that would convert loops and hooks into tape – easier said than done.)* Thinking about obstacles before you start will equip you mentally with the necessary fighting spirit; if you encounter difficulties it will not sap your enthusiasm because you are prepared for setbacks.

6 HOW WILL YOU OVERCOME THESE OBSTACLES?

If you think about this now, it will conserve your energy for the
really unexpected!

 In practice

You may feel all this is very similar to project management. It is.
The major difference is that it is you who gave birth to your
project – it is your idea, therefore you are in control of its
well-being.

The benefits of the six-point approach involve more than
gaining corporate approval. It teaches you how to screen ideas,
how to build team consensus and how to look ahead,
considering both the positive and the likely difficulties. As I am
sure you have observed, some people spend all their time
working on those parts of an idea they like or know best, while
ignoring the rest. This six-point plan ensures that you consider
all the aspects involved in developing an idea.

Remember:

→   The plan works best if you have two or three different
     ideas you wish to develop. Use the techniques above to
     establish which one fits your circumstances best before
     you begin your development.

→   If you are a manager and have to consider several ideas,
     the approach is invaluable. Encourage your team to use
     the plan to analyse the impact of a particular idea
     immediately prior to development.

→   Consider beginning your analysis with a customer.

Case study

A UK electronics engineering company manufactured a high-volume, low-skill product relying on one major domestic customer. The product was threatened by new trends in technology and the company felt it needed to expand its customer base. The company had one strength, its engineering department, staffed with young engineers buzzing with ideas that needed harnessing, and one weakness, its marketing department, which had a poor record.

The manager of the engineering department wrote a paper designed to encourage his department to embrace an innovative culture which, in his own words, was all about: 'Survival. Our market share is threatened, our product price is under pressure, and we find it increasingly difficult to fund the developments demanded by our major customer. There are too many suppliers chasing too few customers. We need a break-out innovation to a) enhance our existing product, and its market, and b) to exploit our skills to take us into a different product, market or technology.'

The manager applied the six-point plan as follows.

1. What is our target area?
(a)   To enhance our existing product and its market
(b)   To exploit our skills to bring about a new product

2. What should be our strategy for getting there?
(a)   Position our existing product in relation to the whole UK communications network
(b)   Widen our market share; consider export
(c)   Evaluate our skills as a business and consider what other product areas would permit us to use them to advantage
(d)   Set up a business unit, flexible, organic, responsive and highly communicative

3.   What resources are needed?

The major resource needed right now is knowledge:

(a) A better understanding of threatening technology

(b) A better understanding of our research department to establish our limits

(c) A better understanding of our marketing function

(d) A better understanding of our clients' needs

4.   Where do we plan to be at specific times?

(a) Set up a business unit within six months

(b) Go and see customers within six months

(c) Bring a new product to the market within two years

5.   What obstacles might there be?

(a) Lack of support from top management

(b) Lack of cooperation from the marketing department

6.   How will they be overcome?

(a) By developing a business case for our MD

(b) By inviting our major customer to a meeting with the MD

(c) By starting informal contacts with Marketing to establish alliances within the department

In fact this company did all the above and was able to produce a new product within eighteen months. They found it easier to market in developing countries rather than on the home front, and started selling to China and South America. Two years later they merged with another European firm and were able to do so on their own terms.

Further resources

Senge, Peter, et al., *The Fifth Discipline Fieldbook*, Nicholas Brealey (1994). Full of tips, techniques and approaches.

Chapter 17

Integrating skills – putting your team together

'We are a pack animal. From earliest times we have used the strength of the group to overcome the weakness of the individual. And that applies as much to business as to sport.'
– TRACEY EDWARDS, YATCHSWOMAN

The object of a team is to integrate a range of skills so as to focus on a common objective. It is a weak team if all its members have the same skill. A football team made up entirely of goalkeepers would not win the league.

There are several techniques for assessing the strengths an individual can bring to a team. The best known is Belbin's Team Roles (see Further Resources). Organisations adopt one of two methods to form teams: either they make a special effort to put people together cross-functionally, pooling resources from all over the business, or they wait until a self-appointed innovator comes along to take on the responsibility of assembling the required people for his or her specific need. The size of your organisation will affect the way it is organised. The larger it is, the more potential for cross-functionality.

WHAT THE EXPERTS SAY

In a remarkable article, Andrall E. Pearson, former President of PepsiCo and previously with McKinsey & Co., outlines the importance of separating the day-to-day operating business from the innovative function (see Further Resources). In other words, he recommends setting up two kinds of organisation within your firm: one that manages, and another that allows ideas to obtain endorsement quickly, the latter staffed by cross-functional teams focused solely on outcomes.

Organisations that do this, such as PepsiCo, 3M and GE, tend to attract like-minded people who are at ease with this kind of culture; putting the team together presents little difficulty.

For example, at 3M L. D. DeSimone, Chairman and CEO, explains that they have three ways of organising people to exploit innovation:

- *Skunkworks* – small groups that quietly pursue new ideas outside the organisational mainstream, the projects spearheaded by employees
- *Traditional development* in which managers and researchers work together to create or improve products
- *Pacing programmes* focused on a small number of products that should bring in profits quickly

3M recognises that, in their large organisation, innovation can arise from a variety of sources, and people will set up or join the group that exploits their strengths best.

A word of caution, though, regarding 'skunkworks'. There is a danger with this formula – if it is the only one followed – that one group breaks away from the rest altogether. This is what happened in the early 1980s when Macintosh computers broke away from Apple. The resulting upheaval upset Apple so much that they had to rethink their structure and strategy, and eventually reinvent themselves. Although, one might argue, this paid off in the end.

→ In practice

Whether they belong to large or small organisations, high-performance teams display the following characteristics:

1. *A shared sense of purpose:* a common mandate, with a strong focus on results, a sense of priorities and clarity about decisions.
2. *Open communications:* people feel free to express their thoughts and feelings; conflicts are brought into the open and resolved. There are no hidden agendas.
3. *Trust and mutual respect:* people value and respect other members of the team. They provide honest feedback.
4. *Shared leadership:* depending on the task, different team members assume leadership. The formal leader acts as coach or mentor to the team.
5. *Effective working procedures:* the team knows how to gather, organise and evaluate information. People plan appropriately.
6. *Building on differences:* the team optimises the different skills, knowledge and strengths of its members. People seek the views of outsiders.
7. *Flexibility and adaptability:* the team views changes or setbacks as opportunities. It reframes its objectives and responds quickly.
8. *Continuous learning:* the team learns from both successes and mistakes and encourages the growth and development of other members.

Try this

If you are uncertain of the people around you, or wonder whether your organisation attracts team players, see whether you can do the following.

CREATE A LEARNING TEAM

As teams learn through a process of trial and error, people need to feel that mistakes are allowed. Neutralise fear of the embarrassment of trying and failing, annihilate the blame culture, share new knowledge by encouraging questions and concerns.

CREATE A PSYCHOLOGICALLY SAFE ENVIRONMENT

Discourage 'defensive reactions' that cover up problems rather than solve them. This is quite challenging. If a person is told they are behaving defensively the likely reaction will be 'Me? Behaving defensively? Certainly not'. You, as leader, need to encourage people to question their own assumptions. You create a role model by questioning your own.

BE ACCESSIBLE

If you want to encourage dialogue, discussions and open communication devoid of defensiveness, be available yourself – not tucked away with your door closed. Set the tone by welcoming people who bring an idea or a problem to you, and do not make them feel inadequate.

Further resources

Belbin, Meredith, *Management Teams. Why They Succeed or Fail*, Heinemann (1981).

Belbin, Meredith, *The Coming Shape of Organisation*, Butterworth-Heinemann (1996).

DeSimone, L, et al., 'How Can Big Companies Keep the Entrepreneurial Spirit Alive', *Harvard Business Review* (November/December 1995).

Pearson, Andrall E., 'Tough-Minded Ways to Get Innovative', *Harvard Business Review* (May/June 1988).

White, Jim, 'Teaming with Talent', *Management Today* (September 1999).

Chapter 18
Friends in high places – identifying a sponsor

'You cannot carry the day by facts alone, you need someone more powerful to take the chance with you and shield you.'
– CHUCK HOUSE, FORMERLY AT HEWLETT-PACKARD

You may be raring to go, armed with the perfect idea and energised with boundless stamina, but you will still need the help of someone else high enough up in your organisation to marshal resources and overcome unknown hurdles.

Consider how, in the eighteenth and nineteenth centuries, even creative geniuses such as Mozart, Gainsborough, Goethe or Capability Brown needed a 'patron', someone who understood their vision, their craft, their difficulties – a friend in high places. It is not so different in organisations today.

A sponsor, the modern version of the patron, ensures that you are getting the resources needed at the appropriate time and finds solutions to the problems raised by your idea. He or she is realistic and tempers the idealistic tendencies of the innovative team, and has enough clout to influence others. The sponsor's judgement is respected.

A sponsor's involvement is invaluable in:

- Accepting or dropping the idea
- Presenting the idea to top management
- Removing bureaucratic barriers
- Releasing resources at the correct time
- Encouraging the team when there are setbacks

In large organisations some form of sponsorship is essential if high-performance teamwork is to be successful. Even in medium-sized and small organisations it is hugely important in developing and supporting the innovative approach. A sponsor tends to be someone more senior than you, who believes in ideas, who has influence with the Board and to whom you have easy access.

How do you go about finding a sponsor? There are some guidelines to consider before you begin your search.

DO'S

Clarity, clarity and more clarity
Who will understand and support you if you demonstrate confusion and lack of commitment? A one-page summary focused on what you want to achieve and the expected outcome will help. Your potential sponsor needs to grasp quickly what you have in mind.

Demonstrate that your idea benefits the company more that it does you
It may sound suspiciously altruistic but the sponsor will be more responsive.

Start small
Involve only one customer initially; it is easier for the sponsor to maintain a dialogue with just one client. If you are successful, the sponsor will broaden the customer base.

Get a team together
Tell your sponsor that you have found people whose skills complement yours and earmark experts who may help you when you encounter problems.

DON'TS

Waste people's time
If you have not done your homework – that is, completed at least some of the preparation outlined in the previous chapters – leave well alone. Sponsors judge people through their deeds, not their words.

Promise the impossible
Sponsors are experienced people. They put their trust in you but they know that difficulties will emerge. Have a great idea, be convincing and display commitment, but keep a sense of realism.

SPOTTING A SPONSOR, AN OPPORTUNITY AND AN INNOVATOR!

It may be that you have not yet had a great idea, but you have the personality and probably the track record to deliver something new. I knew a senior manager who finished his Monday morning briefing meetings with half a dozen problems or opportunities he had noticed that needed solving or looking into. Just to fix them in people's minds, he wrote them on a whiteboard in his office. The list stayed up for the week, while he waited to see 'who caught the ball'. This allowed him to do two things: to identify innovators, and to put himself forward as a sponsor, albeit unofficially.

   This system is common in large organisations when innovators are promoted and given the responsibility for a business unit or some autonomy to deliver new products.

In practice

Look at this chapter from two angles. Could you be a sponsor, or are you looking for one?

If you can be a sponsor:

→ Do people's ideas excite you?

→ Do you have access to resources?

→ Are you respected by your most senior colleagues?

→ Are you a good communicator?

If you are looking for one:

→ Go for someone senior to you

→ Gain his or her respect

→ Listen to his or her advice

→ Keep your sponsor involved and informed

A FINAL THOUGHT

I have a suggestion to make to organisations with access to experienced retired executives. A lot of that experience could be used if these people were invited back, say on a consultancy basis, to serve as sponsors. The benefits are obvious:

- Many executives would like to 'keep a hand in' without the stress and responsibilities of a full-time job.
- The expertise, knowledge, experience and skills of such individuals may have taken many years to acquire. Why lose them when they retire? It is the organisation that will suffer.
- Less experienced individuals and teams would be in a position to learn from the more experienced, unintimidated by rank or seniority.

If you can introduce such a scheme in your firm, why not do so? There's an innovation for you!

Further resources

Pinchot, Gifford, III, *Intrapreneuring*, Harper & Row (1985), in particular Chapter 7.

Chapter 19
Someone who can say no – identifying your customers

*'Qu'est-ce qu'un homme révolté? Un homme qui dit non
(What is a rebel? A man who says no).'*
– ALBERT CAMUS, FRENCH PLAYWRIGHT

*'Point d'argent, point de Suisse, et ma porte était close
(No money, no service, and my door stayed shut).'*
– JEAN RACINE, FRENCH TRAGEDIAN

WHO ARE YOUR CUSTOMERS?

This may appear obvious, but I have found it essential that
in the field of innovation nothing should be taken for
granted. I agree entirely with Peter Drucker, who says *'a
customer is someone who can say "no"…'* This perception
is direct, unambiguous and impossible to argue with. To
think of customers as Drucker does opens up a wide range
of possibilities.

THE BLIND PUBLIC SECTOR

I have observed that this notion is less well received in the public sector. Why? Consider academia. A school leaver frequently receives offers from several universities. I recall the horror engendered a couple of years ago when a handful of such young people *refused* a place at Oxford. This took the academic world completely by surprise, but it should not have done so. A patient has a choice of doctors and can, within the vicinity, 'shop around'. The Civil Service is also open to the market today. There are agencies; there are services contracted out; there is the possibility that if a service becomes inefficient – and today governments have an array of productivity and audit tools – the unit or department in question will be disbanded.

Monopolies are dwindling.

THE COMPLACENT PRIVATE SECTOR

Of course, in the private sector the issue of customers is clearer. Yet there is many a chairman and managing director who thinks their existing customers are there for life. Be warned. Customers are becoming better informed and will choose, or experiment with, what they view as a better deal.

Recall how the fortunes of the giant and highly successful IBM dipped, partly because the creed that 'nobody got fired for buying IBM', combined with an ingrained belief that their range of products was everything the customer needed, led to an arrogant attitude. Competitors seized the moment and taught IBM a painful lesson.

Witness, as I write, British Airways' customer-base defection to the cheaper no-frills airlines.

To summarise, success breeds failure.

In practice

Understanding who your customers are requires thinking beyond the obvious. The obvious is 'someone who buys from me or uses my service'. This concept belongs to the nineteenth century. In the field of innovation, we need to think of a customer as a partner, an individual with whom we form a relationship. As in all relationships, we need to bring to it care, listening skills, an understanding of that person's concerns, an awareness of their successes, and some thought for *their* customers as well. Relationships need to be managed.

This does not entail trying to sell more of existing products but instead giving that customer the value that will make the relationship unique and difficult to sever. Such a relationship breeds loyalty.

Consider also your internal customers. Who are they? Why do they come to you? Would it not be cheaper for them to go elsewhere?

 Try this

➜   Get your team together and list your customers. Select those with whom you have a close relationship. What are the outcomes? What benefits has the relationship brought you? What benefits has the relationship brought them? Could you extend this approach to other customers?

➜   Organise a meeting with your internal customers – if you are in Finance this could be the directors of marketing, procurement or anybody with a budget. Ask them what their key concerns are at present. Discuss how they view the next six months. What trends do they see? Is what you give them what they need? Should you stop doing something? Should you start doing something you do not do already? Should you present material differently? What do they do with the information you give them?

Remember, unless you have identified your customers and understood who they are, your efforts in meeting their needs will be wasted.

Further resources

Drucker, Peter, *Innovation and Entrepreneurship*, Harper & Row (1985).

Chapter 20
Time and communication – the role of management

'Yesbutters don't just kill ideas, they kill entire companies, even industries. Because Yesbutters have all the answers. Yes, but we are too small, yes, but we cannot afford it, yes, but let's wait and see.'
– ADVERTISING POSTER FOR GE IN THE 1980S

'He who does not trust enough will not be trusted.'
– LAO-TZU, CHINESE PHILOSOPHER

This chapter looks at three skills managers need: Understanding Time, Coaching and Communications. If you reflect on this for a second, you will see that all three skills are closely connected and all three are essential in managing innovators. Innovators need your time, your encouragement and clarity in communications.

Consider the following key questions:

- As a manager, how much time do you spend thinking about innovation and about new ways of thinking?
- How do you get the best from your team?

- Who depends on you for what information? And on whom do you depend?

TIME: THE HARE AND THE TORTOISE

Time is sequential, measurable, and in these days of faster communications and transportation time is a management issue more than ever: there is pressure to increase the pace of product development, and a constant requirement for managers to speed up their decision-making and the business processes for which they are responsible.

I once came across a marketing director who used to say, when presented with a new idea, 'If we can't have it in two weeks, don't bother with it.' He did not understand that some ideas take time to develop. He was expecting difficulties, not solutions.

And yet he was not entirely misguided! Of all the skills a manager needs to master, time as a concept is the most difficult. Time is ambiguous. While speed can be desirable, rushing to judge or evaluate a brand-new idea is the best way of killing it. Wise managers, working for wise organisations, allow time for ideas to be explored before passing judgement. Wise managers change time gears depending on the situation they are facing.

 In practice

To learn to manage the relationship between time and innovation, consider the following:

→ How many hours per week have you spent considering innovation? Was it time well spent? If not, why not?

→ How many new ways of working have you initiated in the past year? Could there have been more?

→ How comfortable are you in standing up to your

management and informing them that there are delays with a project?

➜   Let somebody in your team choose a promising idea for development. Keep a log of how long it takes.

➜   How do you run meetings? Let someone else run one. Could something be changed for the better?

COACHING THE MOTIVATED

When managing innovators, keep in mind that what drives them is a desire to deliver something better than what has been available before. Consequently, they set very high standards for themselves, strive for excellence, and define their own goals. Managing is not quite the right term for what you should be doing. Coaching is more appropriate.

John Whitmore – formerly a sports coach, now a management coach – created this model based on the acronym **GROW**. **G** stands for Goal, **R** for Reality, **O** for Opportunity and **W** for Will.

 Try this

Use GROW at an early meeting with your innovator, when he or she wants to present you with an idea. Like all good coaches, you should be accessible and ask open-ended questions. For example, your dialogue could go as follows:

'What have you got there, John? What's the Goal?'

When you have heard the idea, you continue with 'Do you think we could do it? Have we got the people? What's in it for you?', thus checking the Reality.

When you have listened to your innovator's reply, you pursue Opportunity with 'And who would want it? Have you talked to potential customers?'

And your final questions investigate Will: 'When can we start? What do you need from me?'

This type of dialogue is an innovator's dream. Note that you have taken the time to hear John's points and that the exchange contains no 'Yes, but', rather an implicit 'Yes, and' to give this initial idea a chance of survival.

COMMUNICATION

There are three angles that you need to consider here: connections, rejections and setbacks.

CONNECTIONS

Innovative organisations understand the need for people to connect with each other; they bring down barriers through workshops, conferences, away-days, social events or clubs. Your managerial role at the birth of an innovative project is to encourage people to talk easily, to make contact, free of bureaucratic interference. Your task at this point is to speed up communications – here we overlap with the section on time above.

REJECTIONS

This is frequently overlooked. Rejection happens when the green light cannot be given to an idea. Many managers fail to explain their reasons, and the consequences are serious:

- Innovators lose trust in their managers. Eventually they cease to trust the entire organisation and they leave.
- No learning takes place. People do not improve since they do not know what to improve.

SETBACKS

Every innovation suffers setbacks. Many fail. How can you try something new without risking failure? As a manager, imbued with a culture of 'getting it right first time', how do you react? Pause to consider this checklist:

- Do you conduct debriefing sessions devoid of blame syndrome?
- Do you measure and monitor systematically with the innovative team what you have learnt?
- Are people resolved not to repeat the errors noted?
- Are failures used as signposts to point the way to growth?

People who have tried and failed have acquired the skills and knowledge to try again. The manager's role is to understand this. As Thomas Edison is reputed to have said after his thousandth attempt to find a material for the incandescent filament of an electric lamp, *'I now know a thousand ways which do not work. One day I will find one that does.'* And he did.

 Try this

- → Think of ways in which you could transform existing knowledge to reflect new knowledge and insight and present it to *your* manager.
- → If you have to reject an idea, tell your innovator or innovative team what your reasons are. Confirm that they have understood. Perhaps you are able to tell them that the idea cannot be developed now but that you will make a note of it for a later date.
- → Go and have a drink with the innovative team when things are not going well. If an idea has failed, discuss other possibilities together.

Further resources

Garvin, David A., 'Building a Learning Organisation', *Harvard Business Review* (July/August 1993).

O'Hare, Mark, *Innovate! How to Gain and Sustain Competitive Advantage*, Blackwell (1988), in particular pp. 177–8.

Pinchot, Gifford, III, *Intrapreneuring*, Harper & Row (1985), in particular pp. 172–3 and 224–8.

Senge, Peter, *The Fifth Discipline*, Doubleday (1990), in particular Chapters 2 and 15.

Chapter 21
Root to crown – managing senior management

'By working faithfully eight hours a day, you may eventually get to be a boss and work twelve hours a day'
– ROBERT FROST, POET

'The longer the title, the less important the job'
– GEORGE MCGOVERN, AMERICAN POLITICIAN

*'Along this tree
From root to crown
Ideas flow up
And vetoes down'*   – ATTRIBUTED TO A UNILEVER EXECUTIVE

A REMINDER TO SENIOR MANAGERS

What is the role of senior management in innovation? To ease the path for innovators, in effect to turn possible ideas into reality; to enable them to reach development *and* implementation. It follows that senior management needs to demonstrate certain qualities:

- Listening abilities. There will be lots of ideas; some are impractical and unrealistic while others will have the potential for success.

- Coaching abilities. To pursue the potentially success-ful ideas, the senior manager will go beyond encouragement. Like a coach, he or she will engage in a discussion that makes the innovator think beyond the concept stage. The dialogue will be posi-tive; for example: How can this be done? What will be the benefits of developing this now?

- Senior management keeps a foot firmly planted in the 'ethos' of the company. This will compensate for the weakness of innovators, who will sometimes come up with ideas that do not fit the mission of the organisa-tion they are working for. The senior manager is the guardian of that mission.

MANAGING THE MANAGERS

My stance here is that at best you may not be sure who you are dealing with; at worst you may have to deal with a non-sympathetic manager.

Let us examine the first instance. What can you learn about your boss?

BEST-CASE SCENARIO

- Find out what his or her aims and values are, what they want for themselves and what they want for others. Is a step up the ladder more important than initiating something new? Do they have a track record of innovation – sponsoring or initiating a new product or service?

- Can you identify their strengths and weaknesses? Do they have new ideas? What do they like and what do they not want to do? Check your perception with others.

- How do they prefer to work? Do they favour

informal one-to-one chats, e-mail communication or more formal paper presentations? Do they consider a problem *and* its solution? Do they mull things over? Do they like to talk things over with peers?

- What pressures are they under at present? What objectives and targets have they been given? How much autonomy are they granted?

Now, how can you use what you have learnt?

- Are you clear about what motivates you? Is there a match with your boss? If not, can you work on this?
- Are you also clear about your strengths and weaknesses? Do you balance your boss's profile or are you more or less a replica?
- How do you like to communicate? Can you tell your boss? If there is a mismatch could you offer a way round it and review it together after, say, three months?
- Can you remove sources of conflict for your boss? Offer solutions? Give her or him time to think over proposals?

One golden rule: *Never surprise or denigrate your boss in front of his or her own management.*

WORST-CASE SCENARIO

Your boss is inaccessible

- Send him or her an e-mail with a short summary of what you want to talk about.
- Use the old adage 'It is easier to ask for forgiveness than for permission' – within reason!
- Tell him or her. They may not know that you need regular exchanges.

He or she does not keep you informed
- Tell them.
- Think of the wider ramifications. It may be to protect *you*.
- Use other sources.
- Show an example: keep them informed. Make sure they have everything they need.
- Stick to deadlines. Show that you are reliable.

He or she has a closed mind regarding anything new
- Always accompany a new approach by showing 'what's in it for them'. Demonstrate how *they* will benefit from your idea.
- Do not give up. Persistence here counts.
- If your organisation has an open-door policy, use it: in the circumstances, that's what your boss's boss is all about.
- Ask for a transfer!

And generally, use your appraisal system. That is what it is there for. Prepare your grievance with examples and an objective analysis of the situation.

 In practice

This whole chapter is about ideas to put into practice. So go ahead and practise them!

Further resources

Drucker, Peter, *Management: Tasks, Responsibilities, Practices*, Heinemann (1974), in particular Chapter 61.

Roebuck, Chris, *Effective Communications*, Video Arts-Marshall Publishing (undated), in particular Chapter 5.

Chapter 22
Feedback – involving your customers

'Unless you have 100% customer satisfaction – and I
don't mean that they are just satisfied, I mean that they
are excited about what you are doing – you have to
improve; and if you have 100% customer satisfaction, you
have to make sure that you listen in case they change ...
so you can change with them.'
– HORST SCHULZE, FORMER PRESIDENT AND COO OF
THE RITZ-CARLTON HOTEL COMPANY

Your customers are the reason you are in business.
Everyone in employment sells something to someone: a
doctor sells health, a priest the word of God, a university
professor knowledge. Customers are our most precious
asset. In Part 1 we looked at how customers can be a reliable
source of ideas. Yet many organisations are reluctant to
involve customers when they begin the development stage.

My own experience shows that managers have three
fears:

- That involving a customer as they embark on the
  development stage is a sign of weakness
- That the customer may not accept entering in a sole-
  sourcing relationship

- That there is a risk that the embryonic idea will be leaked to a competitor

GET YOUR CUSTOMERS INVOLVED EARLY ON

A natural reaction of many managers is to begin development only after all problems and issues have been resolved, but this delay risks grave consequences: the morale and enthusiasm of the innovative team dip; the customers' patience is tried to the point where they may go to the competition or lose interest; and the link between idea generation and revenue is lost. Continued customer involvement maintains channels of communication and translates customer needs into products quickly and efficiently. Rather than showing weakness, it demonstrates to the customer your ability to listen, your flexibility and commitment to succeed. In return you will earn their loyalty.

SOLE SOURCING

This is an issue that will not arise if you maintain a continuous dialogue with customers. Keep in mind that your customers already have several suppliers. They will prefer to enter into a relationship with a supplier who listens and helps solve their problems. It gives them exclusivity. They like to know that they are part of the elite, the select few. It flatters them to be consulted.

COMPETITION

In business there is always the possibility that the competition will beat you to the finishing line. But remember that the competition comprises people like you, who have managers like yours and a whole infrastructure that is similar to your own. For them to gear up and overtake you will require great effort. You have the advantage of being first, so make sure you capitalise on it.

However, keep one factor in mind. Ask yourself whether your idea is easy to copy. This is the first question I put to clients when they submit an innovation to me. The more complex the innovation is, the lower the risk of copying. If your innovation entails changes in your business systems it will be less attractive to competitors, who will not be inclined to make radical changes.

I can illustrate this with the example of J. Sainsbury, the British food chain retailer. In the mid-1990s its rival, Tesco, introduced a loyalty card, an idea which Sainsbury pooh-poohed. A couple of years later a contrite Sainsbury was forced to admit the success of the loyalty card and intro-duce its own. For a while Tesco supplanted Sainsbury in profits and market share. But Sainsbury has now regained lost ground. The loyalty card was quite easy to copy.

 Try this

Once you have selected your targeted customer, or group of customers, have defined the goal they need to achieve, have written your business plan and acquired the necessary resources, then you need to:

→ Keep lines of communication with your customers open. It shows that you are tuning in to their real concerns.

→ Monitor each stage with the customer. Test your assumptions. Ensure they are aligned with reality of the customer's need.

→ Adapt and modify your idea as you receive feedback from your customer.

→ Keep your mind open: narrow thinking will limit the rele-vance of your innovation.

→   Hold periodic innovation presentations for managers.
These are not undeclared invitations to shoot down the
project, but opportunities for synergistic efforts to improve
it.

→   Invite and welcome the customers' experts if you get
stuck. They have been in this situation before, they have
seen the problems before, and they know how best to fix
them.

Further resources

O'Hare, Mark, *Innovate! How to Gain and Sustain Competitive
Advantage*, Blackwell (1988), in particular Chapter 6.
Rydz, John S., *Managing Innovation*, Ballinger (1986), in particu-
lar Chapters 4 and 8.
Seybold, Patricia S., 'Get Inside the Lives of Your Customers',
Harvard Business Review (May 2001).

Chapter 23

What will happen to your idea? – the innovation curve

'It is not the man in your life that counts. It's the life in your man.'
– MAE WEST, ACTRESS

'Life is a process of becoming a combination of states we have to go through. Where people fail is that they wish to choose a state and remain in it.'
– ANAÏS NIN, WRITER

'In the field of observation, chance favours the prepared mind.'
– LOUIS PASTEUR, CHEMIST

Reflect on your personal experience. If you work on something novel, do you usually expect success all the way or do you expect there to be setbacks? In my own experience the answer depends on who I put the question to. Managers tend to expect a trouble-free curve and seem surprised when setbacks emerge; innovators expect setbacks and are surprised when there are only a few.

THE REALITY OF INNOVATIONS

Most new, untested ideas go through the following five stages:

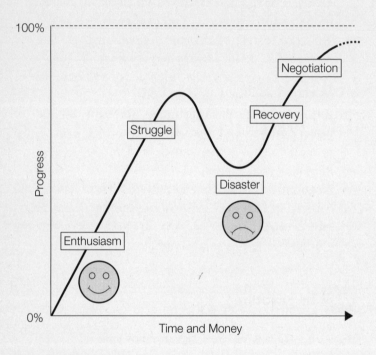

The innovation curve

- **Enthusiasm** gets the team going. The project has been given the go-ahead; confidence of success is high. Riding on this euphoria, progress is fast.
- **Struggle** now sets in. Things are more difficult than was first thought, but morale is still high because these obstacles were anticipated (see Chapter 16). If you have a sponsor, he or she will evaluate what other resources you might need and will set to work to release them. If you don't, your manager will fill this role.
- **Disaster** strikes. Something totally unexpected

happens. Experienced sponsors and managers have been expecting this. The innovative team's confidence is shaken. It will need all the support the manager or sponsor can give, which means more than comforting words. You can measure a firm's ability to foster and manage innovation now. The moment has come when synergies work at their best: customers' input, experts' knowledge and experience, managers' and sponsors' actions.

- **Recovery** begins once customers and experts have been consulted and their advice absorbed. But progress is slower than anticipated and some deadlines may have lapsed.
- **Negotiation**. Struggles and disasters have changed the original idea. It may be short of your expectations, it may exceed them. Either way, are you and your team going to accept its final shape?

 In practice

There are three lessons worth expanding on here.

ACCEPTANCE

It is crucial that as a manager and innovator you understand and accept these five stages. The most important is, of course, disaster, and surviving it. Many innovations fail at this stage because managers find it difficult to face the unexpected. Organisations devote enormous resources to preventing disasters: they lay down procedures and institute rigid control systems which make managers ill equipped to face the unknown. Consequently many abandon projects at this stage and, in their mind, they equate new ideas with disaster. This is quite common in large organisations.

KEEP TO YOUR TEAM

Sometimes managers change the team at the disaster stage. This is a recipe for further disaster as the newcomers will not have the commitment of the first team, nor the experience the team has, by now, acquired. When this occurs, the project fizzles out, wasting resources. This happens frequently in the public sector, where a culture of rapid job changes is the norm.

DID YOU SAY EXPERTS?

Finally, note that experts are brought in at the crucial stage as problem-solvers. Experts have problems 'unlearning' their trade – if you try something new, you are challenging their expertise. So if you consult them too early a typical reaction might be: 'I wouldn't try this, if I were you; we tried it some time ago and it didn't work.' If, however, you bring them in at the right time, their contribution will be invaluable precisely because they know more about the subject than anyone else. They can fix it. Remember the old adage: 'Experts should be on tap, not on top'.

 Try this

If you are starting to develop an idea, be prepared for severe setbacks. As both manager and innovator you can:

TOLERATE MISTAKES AND FAILURES

They are inherent to any innovation. Learn from them. From the unexpected some other great idea could emerge. Take the example of the sweet delicacy from northern France known as *bêtises de Cambrai*, which resulted from the inattention of a confectioner's apprentice. The mixture he was meant to supervise burnt, but he and his master tasted and liked the minty mass at the bottom of the cauldron. It has been a bestseller for over 100 years.

LEARN

If you are not currently developing an idea, reflect on past experiences and jot down what happened.

→ What was really unexpected?
→ Did you overcome the problem?
→ Who helped you?
→ What was the morale of your team like during this period?
→ Did you keep the dialogue going with your customers?
→ How did they react?

Case study

I once attended a very high-powered meeting in a multinational firm, and asked the question 'What will happen to your idea?'. There was a silence, during which someone entered the room. 'Don't mind me,' he said as he spotted an empty chair, 'just carry on. What were you saying?' I repeated the question. He got up, went to the flip chart, drew a perfect curve plotted again the axes of time and effort, and punctuated his contribution with the satisfied remark, 'This is how things are done here.' I noted, 'You must be a senior manager.' 'Yes,' he replied, 'I am the managing director.' 'And no one tells you when things go wrong,' I said.

There was a pause. He looked around the room. People were avoiding his gaze. 'I think you may be right,' he admitted. 'We need to discuss this.' We did, and soon discovered why this world-famous company did not score highly for its innovative powers: the most senior person inspired fear rather than respect. Accordingly setbacks were not reported. As a

result he was convinced that every new project succeeded
and could not see why experimentation was necessary.

Further resources

Foster, Richard, *Innovation*, Summit Books (1986), in particular
Chapters 1 and 2.

Lynch, Dudley, and Paul L. Kordis, *Strategy of the Dolphin*,
Hutchinson Business Books (1988), in particular Chapters 2
and 6.

Chapter 24

When the going gets tough – dealing with setbacks and conflicts

'The fastest way to succeed is to double your failure rate.'
– THOMAS WATSON, SR, FOUNDER OF IBM

'When the going gets tough, the tough get going.'
– JOSEPH P. KENNEDY, US AMBASSADOR AND FATHER OF
JOHN F. KENNEDY

I have mentioned setbacks several times in this section, but they deserve closer attention. It stands to reason that if you try to develop something new it may not succeed in the way you intended; or it may fail altogether. It would be unrealistic to believe otherwise. Therefore organisations need to accept setbacks – even failures.

Conflict, in the context of this chapter, means conflict within the team. Managers in enlightened organisations avoid conflict. But if you are confronted with conflict, how do you handle it?

PREPARE FOR SETBACKS

The first step is awareness. The second is to plan. If you plan, you keep some energy and resources in reserve to face the unexpected. Chapters 16 and 23 give you specific tools to enable you to plan for setbacks. Rather than reiterate preventive tools, this chapter will look at a situation you may have to face. If you were facing a setback right now and had not planned for it, what could you do?

 Try this

Consider these questions:
1. What are the manifestations of this setback?
2. How are you handling it?
3. What effect does it have on your team and customer?
4. Can you identify a setback owner?

Armed with some answers, check your perceptions with your team. This is important because:
→ It limits the damage to a specific set of problems
→ It opens up discussions with one or two team members, thus avoiding cover-ups and defensive attitudes.

When you have identified a setback owner, discuss how the problem can be overcome. At this stage, concentrate on *what* can be done, not *why* it happened. (Keep the why until the project is almost completed; see Chapter 34.)

Once the problem is fully understood (but not before), involve your sponsor and customer. By enlarging the sphere of the problem, you are increasing the possibilities of solving it.

DEALING WITH CONFLICTS

Creating a culture that accepts setbacks means, for some organisations, changing traditional mindsets, by fostering collaboration over personal competition. Innovative organisations understand that the sharing of information, the analysis of mistakes and the freedom to express thoughts are key factors in innovation.

Conflicts happen when people have not quite made the shift from focusing on individual performance to focusing on team performance, a shift that requires a move from individual to mutual accountability. The foundation of that mutual accountability is trust. While this is a fairly straightforward concept to grasp, in practice there are some guidelines for you, the manager, to consider.

 Try this

EARN EMPATHY

Have you experienced a setback, a resounding failure, something that caused you to learn the hard way? Tell your team. People come to respect and trust someone who, like themselves, can show that they are fallible.

Culture shifts only happen when managers set themselves up as role models.

COLLABORATE, DON'T CONTROL

At the end of each day or week, do you conduct an informal debrief to discuss successes and problems? In such sessions, successes are acknowledged and problems are openly discussed in order to reach a solution, to learn and to plan the next stage.

ACKNOWLEDGE FUZZINESS

Encourage your team to recognise the fuzziness of a situation. Instead of avoiding assumptions and hidden agendas, organise a meeting where everyone's point of view is aired while others listen. Collect all the information on flip charts. Then select the issues that people feel are the most important and focus the discussion on 'How can we minimise the effects of/clarify/avoid this situation in future?'

Further resources

Farson, Richard, and Ralph Keyes, 'The Failure-Tolerant Leader', *Harvard Business Review* (August 2002).

Katzenbach, Jon R., and Douglas K. Smith, *The Wisdom of Teams*, McGraw-Hill (1998), in particular Chapter 3.

Chapter 25
Providing the framework – supporting creative and innovative people

'Making the effort to be a leader of creative people and learning to follow them signal both leadership competence and the understanding that such work comes from the heart and not from a management handbook.'
– MAX DE PREE, BUSINESS LEADER

'The beautiful souls are they that are universal, open and ready for all things.'
– MICHEL DE MONTAIGNE, ESSAYIST

Creative and innovative people appear in many guises. Traditionally associated with the arts, they also feature, of course, in the sciences, and in every kind of organisational structure. But for all their talent, they are not easy to manage, and do not make the best employees.

CREATORS

History abounds with creative people – Shakespeare, Galileo, Mozart, Einstein and Newton are the most often cited by people I ask for examples. They offer us profiles that can help us understand similar people.

Think of Shakespeare, who embodies the creative type in a business environment – someone who had to deal with the frustrations and routine of running a commercial enterprise, a theatre, and who, at short notice, had to produce plays, facing deadlines, shortage of cash, last-minute changes of cast, and inspirational moments alternating with creative blockages. The pressures he faced are similar to those of a copywriter working in an advertising agency.

Glancing at the names above, you will note that creative people tend to work on their own. They do not create organisations – like innovators. Innovators need the resources – knowledge, expertise, power – that organisations possess (although we must be careful to avoid stereotyping with little empirical evidence).

Creative people prize freedom of action above all: not for them close supervision and working to routine objectives. Yet to succeed they also need boundaries and known limits.

Several creative people have commented on their need to forget about the problem they are working on. They believe (and their results confirm) that trusting one's unconscious is crucial. Philosopher Bertrand Russell puts it best: '*I have found that if I have to write upon some rather difficult topic, the best plan is to think about it with very great intensity – the greatest intensity of which I am capable – for a few hours or days, and at the end of that time give orders, so to speak, that the work is to proceed underground. After some months I would return consciously to the topic and find that the work had been done.*' To put it succinctly, they need time to forget.

They also work best within a framework. It may sound paradoxical, but if there are no deadlines, if there is complete freedom, creative people flounder. All the creativity techniques I know have rules and time limits. These parameters are there to free the mind and, simultaneously, to harness it towards a goal.

INNOVATORS

As we defined them in Chapter 2, innovators are hard working. The adage '1 per cent inspiration and 99 per cent perspiration' applies to them. Innovators are focused and committed to success. They build on their strengths and look for opportunities that will enhance and use these strengths, taking measured, well-defined risks. They will not jeopardise their entire organisation on the strength of just one idea. Innovators need recognition. Their source of energy is the knowledge that their ideas are successful. Innovators need resources and become impatient when others – their own management in particular – do not grasp their vision. Generalists rather than specialists, they know a little about a lot of things and like to move about. Consequently they flourish if the job gets them to move cross-functionally.

 In practice

Supporting creative and innovative people first of all requires an organisation that understands how the creative process is fostered. Here are a few pointers for managers:

→ Try to structure your organisation so that it is free of bureaucracy, with lean, hierarchical structures and a clear reporting system

→ Implement adequate rewards systems

→ Aim to establish a track record of innovations

→ Make decisions on who will head a project on an individual basis

➜   Promote innovation from within rather than relying on
outsiders, whether acquisitions or consultants

Further resources

Drucker, Peter, *Innovation and Entrepreneurship*, Harper & Row
(1985), in particular Chapters 10 and 13.
Koestler, Arthur, *The Act of Creation*, Hutchinson (1964).

Part 3:
Implementation –
getting your innovation
to market

Chapter 26
Not just a bonus – reward and recognition

'Entrepreneurs are the most boring dinner companions I know. All they want to talk about is their ventures. They never want to talk about anything interesting like, for example, me.'
– PETER DRUCKER, MANAGEMENT CONSULTANT, QUOTED BY GIFFORD PINCHOT

'Genius, all over the world, stands hand in hand, and one shock of recognition runs the whole circle round.'
– HERMAN MELVILLE, NOVELIST

How do you reward innovators? What do you recognise?

Most firms have not devised a reward system for their innovative people. The classic mode of reward is either promotion or a financial bonus, neither of which motivates innovators.

Managers and organisations need to acknowledge their innovators publicly. Innovators want their talents, efforts and achievements noticed. This is one of their sources of motivation.

Their *talents* involve spotting a need or a gap in the market.

Their *efforts* are evident in their determination to succeed, to overcome setbacks.

And their *achievements* are measured in the implementation, when the innovation is used, if it is a service or procedure, or bought, if it is a product.

Let us first examine the pitfalls of traditional methods of reward.

PROMOTION

Promotion is dangerous because, for the innovator, it entails adhering more closely to the company's procedures, procedures that the innovator has successfully challenged. Innovators break rules and, as long as they are monitored, they are 'allowed' to do so. Promotion removes that freedom.

Promotion tends to involve managing people. Innovators are interested in ideas, not people, at least not in the sense of fostering and understanding them, and spending time in meetings. Innovators make poor managers of people.

NOT JUST A BONUS

No one dislikes receiving a financial bonus, but money is not the main motivator for innovators. To put it crudely, innovators will not come up with an idea, fight for it and stick with it to the bitter end simply because you throw money at them.

One of the dangers of this form of reward is that the person rewarded leaves soon afterwards. This is one of the troubles with middle management in merchant banks, which have a lot of good people at this level who try to implement better customer value, occasionally successfully. They learn the formula: If I succeed, I double my salary. Then, having notched up a success, they leave after two or three years to work for a competitor. The cycle starts again and everyone loses. If, as I have stressed before, your clients are your best asset, your own people come a very close second. Read the case study below.

 In practice

The best option is to ask people what they want, as demonstrated by the case study at the end of this chapter. You will be surprised by how inexpensive what people want can be.

In my experience, these are the rewards people appreciate most:

→   Freedom to do the job. Less supervision, and if possible a discretionary budget enabling them to get embryonic ideas off the ground.

→   A sympathetic managerial structure, ideally one that is separate from the day-to-day management of the business. This implies no unnecessary bureaucratic barriers, no heavy-handed financial interference early on, easy access to one manager, or sponsor, and freedom to tap into the organisation's knowledge and know-how.

→   An organisational recognition system. In some cases this may be a fellowship, in others the recipient's name will simply be pinned to a noticeboard with a brief description of what they have achieved. As a result that person receives certain privileges – for example, more time off with the family, a better computer or an assignment abroad.

→   No penalties or scapegoats if there is failure, simply the opportunity to try again.

Try this

Sit down with your team and ask them what they need. It's that easy!

Case study

I was talking once to a group of senior civil servants, each of whom was typically in charge of several hundred staff. We had been discussing recognition and reward, a difficult issue in the Civil Service, as the scope for manoeuvre is limited. One member of the group – let's call him Humphrey – offered to illustrate this point.

He had been put in charge of creating two new departments out of one, to separate two quite distinct and pretty well unrelated functions. Several hundred thousand personnel were involved. Besides managing the logistics of the situation, several innovative actions were required to implement the change.

The changes went through successfully, on budget and on schedule. Soon afterwards, Humphrey attended a meeting chaired by the Prime Minister. At one point the PM addressed Humphrey, who, up until then, had been sitting at the back of the room. 'You have done a very good job here, Humphrey; really a splendid effort. I am sure we are all very grateful.' The PM turned to the ministers present. 'How can we reward him?' There were blank faces all around and much shuffling of feet, but everyone knew that the PM meant business.

'May I make a suggestion, Prime Minister?' said Humphrey.

'Of course. What is it?'

'I would like a new carpet in my office.'

Astonishment all round. 'What a good idea. See that he gets a good carpet,' replied the PM, her mind already on the next item on the agenda.

A few weeks later Humphrey invited me to his office, and met me personally at the lift. At his office door he instructed me to take my shoes off. I had not expected this but complied. As I did so, Humphrey opened the door, to reveal a superb carpet stretching throughout his large office. Colour, texture and thickness combined to give a luxurious feel to an otherwise unremarkable room. 'Isn't it wonderful?' he said. In one corner of the office I noticed a square foot of floor left bare but for a dark linoleum covering. 'This is how it was before; an improvement, don't you think?'

Humphrey had received the recognition he felt he deserved, and which indeed he did deserve. He was well satisfied.

Further resources

There is very little on this subject. Although not strictly dealing with innovation, Frederick Herzberg's work on motivation is worth reading again.

Herzberg, Frederick, 'One More Time: How Do You Motivate Employees?', *Harvard Business Review* (September/October 1987).

Pinchot, Gifford, III, *Intrapreneuring*, Harper & Row (1985), in particular Chapters 9 and 10.

Chapter 27
Compromise – adjusting the idea

'Great is the art of beginning, but greater is the art of ending.'
– HENRY WADSWORTH LONGFELLOW, POET

'Adversity reveals genius, prosperity conceals it.'
– HORACE, POET AND SATIRIST

This is it. You have now finished the development stage and are entering the implementation phase. Your project is following the curve described in Chapter 23. You have encountered setbacks which have engendered new insights. The end result is that your idea may not quite be as you first envisaged; it is perhaps not quite so grand, or perhaps its scope is beyond what you originally conceived. You need to adapt your mind to the current situation and adjust the idea to the circumstances.

ADAPTING TO THE IDEA

Novelists often say that at some stage in a novel the characters they have created frequently take over and they, the authors, have to follow the characters. The same applies to innovators. Once the idea has formed, it tends to take over. The innovator has to adjust, to follow – and to improve.

In most cases you will receive feedback from customers, input from experts, guidance from your management and insights from your team members, all of which will transform your project. Can you let go of your original goal and accept that your project has reached maturity? It is important that you do so; if not, you will feel frustrated and, rather than looking to the future with confidence, you will look back with resentment.

ADJUSTING THE IDEA

In Chapter 23 the innovation curve reached a point labelled 'Compromise'. When and how does this happen? The process is gradual, of course, but there comes a time when experimentation ceases and implementation begins, when you take your innovation to the marketplace.

 In practice

This is a critical moment when failures may occur. Why should there be failures at this late stage? Because the innovative team and the management have overlooked certain factors:

→   Complexity instead of simplicity
     Influenced by the problems you have had to solve to get your innovation so far, has the idea become too complicated for its target customers? Are they ready for such sophistication? Will lengthy customer training now be required as you introduce your innovation?

→   Marketing
     Who is marketing your innovation? Do they understand what it is? Do they grasp how different your idea is from

the competition? Have they had first-hand experience of it?

➜ Manufacturing issues

Have you and your sponsor given enough warning to the manufacturing side of the business to give them time to prepare? Is there a quality control programme in place?

➜ Legal issues

Did you and your sponsor look into the legal implications *before* you reached this stage?

The case of Enron illustrates the last point. We are told that, in their zeal to promote their key personnel, Enron top management empowered one such employee, Lou Pai, to launch a power-trading business. Unfortunately no one at Enron had checked the true state of so-called recently deregulated markets. The deregulation was such that traditional utilities were favoured over private enterprises such as Lou Pai was engaged in. Enron lost millions.

 Try this

If any of these factors impinge, you still have time to adjust your innovation, and compromise if need be. Accept your findings, adjust your thinking, make small modifications, follow up on early feedback, and test your perceptions with other potential customers.

Further resources

I would be delighted to hear from any reader with good references on this subject.

Chapter 28
Taking the plunge – the launch audit

'There are two golden rules for an orchestra: start together and finish together. The public doesn't give a damn what goes on in between.'
– SIR THOMAS BEECHAM, CONDUCTOR

'What we call the beginning is often the end. And to make an end is to make a beginning. The end is where we start from.'
– T. S. ELIOT, POET

How well do you implement innovative ideas? Implementation here means that the idea has been developed and is ready to be used by, or sold to, customers. You can reduce the likelihood of potential mistakes at this stage if you follow these guidelines.

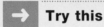 **Try this**

DO'S

START SMALL

Test your innovation on a small and limited market, otherwise you will not have the time or flexibility to make the adjustments and changes that most new ideas need to succeed. The necessary changes can only be made at this stage if the modifications required are fairly modest.

INSTIL CREDIBILITY

If you believe in your idea, be seen to be the first to use it. How can you sell the concept if you are not obviously delighted with it yourself?

PLAN FOR SETBACKS – AGAIN

Although you have been planning all the time, the risk of potential mistakes remains. No system of innovation has yet been designed to produce 100 per cent success. Keep in mind that you may have to tackle two sets of problems: day-to-day ones and fundamental ones.

Deal with each day-to-day problem as it emerges, before it snowballs into something unmanageable.

Fundamental problems can be more difficult to detect. If the planning and evaluation stages have been done thoroughly you will have a strategic statement of the customer value inherent in your idea. Use it to re-examine the assumptions that were made, modify them accordingly or abandon the project.

REWARD THE WHOLE TEAM

Everybody involved in your project deserves praise, from the most junior to the most senior person. Recognition is not just the correct gesture, it is a source of empowerment *pour encourager les autres.*

DON'TS

DON'T INNOVATE FOR THE FUTURE

To be successful an idea must be applicable today. People must be able to see what benefit it has and want to use it; it must radiate a sense of urgency.

In my early thirties, shortly after my parents died, I decided to write a will. I started by telling my lawyer, 'If I follow in my parents' footsteps, I'll die in my late fifties. By that time I'll have accumulated X amount of money which I will leave to ...' He interrupted me. 'Mrs Redway, you do not write a will for twenty years hence. You write it for the present. If you get knocked down by a bus as you leave my office today, what do you have to leave to whom?'

The implementation of an innovation works according to the same principles.

DON'T EMBARK ON ELABORATE MARKET RESEARCH

Sooner rather than later *you* must try your idea out. One of the most important aspects of successful innovation is to find ways of testing ideas with limited risk, but also without compromising the idea itself. This means experimenting directly with the market. The market presents many unknowns that can be discovered only by trial and error. Innovators need to find and develop customers; impersonal market research does not fulfil this need. Professional market research organisations will not come up with the information the innovation team needs. Members of the team must talk to customers to obtain accurate first-hand feedback on the quality of their product.

DON'T CHANGE YOUR TEAM

In particular, don't change your key people. It is a common mistake, for example in the public services, to promote someone or move them to a different job before the final stages of implementation of an innovation. If you change people you will not get the commitment that a new idea needs to survive a launch. Indeed, it may never be implemented. Changing personnel risks losing control of budget, schedule, commitment and staff responsibility.

 In practice

→ Identify potential customers. Select one or two and work directly with them.

→ Do your *own* market research. Select a few customers, demonstrate your product and get face-to-face feedback.

→ Keep a note of customers' reactions. Listen carefully to them. What you learn may change any aspect of your idea, from development to marketing.

→ Remain flexible. If your customers need modifications to your product, or any other part of your plans, make them.

→ Keep exploring and experimenting with customers. Find new ways of presenting your idea. Produce a brochure describing what is different about your product – speed of delivery, replacement guaranteed, ease of application, greater reliability, and so on.

→ Ask selected customers how they would sell the idea. What special feature attracts them?

➡ Will modifications delay the launch of the product? Are you keeping your management informed? Do they have a different view? Do they still support you?

➡ If you have to abandon the idea, get your team together socially. Ask them what lessons you can all learn. Record them.

➡ If you succeed, celebrate. Again, determine the lessons to be learnt, the unexpected contingencies, and record them.

Case study

3M began selling Post-It notes through an advertising campaign in four American cities. Unfortunately they did not issue samples and potential clients did not understand the benefits. The results were disastrous: no one bought the notes. But once Art Fry and a colleague began personally meeting clients and demonstrating the product the customers were hooked.

Further resources

Drucker, Peter, *Innovation and Entrepreneurship*, Harper & Row (1985), in particular Chapter 11.

Chapter 29
The test run – making it work

'Look at the end of work, contrast
The petty done, the undone vast,
This present of theirs with the hopeful past.'
– ROBERT BROWNING, POET

'The new circumstances under which we are placed call
for new words, new phrases, and for the transfer of old
words to new objects.'
– THOMAS JEFFERSON, AMERICAN STATESMAN

You are now very close to full implementation. At this point most organisations run a pilot, or a first exposure with a customer. Here again there are dangers, some of which can be avoided. You need to consider your resources and how you can harness them, your pricing strategy, and potential partners.

RESOURCES

There is no time like now to pull everyone together. You are now testing not only your innovation but the whole infrastructure of your organisation. This is your last chance to ascertain whether the effort can be sustained before full-scale implementation in the marketplace.

THE TEAM

Make sure that everyone from your team is involved, for two reasons. If something goes wrong, they know better than anyone why, and how to fix it. They know the innovation as they would their own child. If, on the other hand, everything goes well, they must share in the success and recognition from colleagues. This is their first justly merited reward.

I meet many disillusioned employees who have been involved in an innovation but, because they have been obliged to change projects, are not invited to participate in this crucial pilot phase. In the best of cases they hear second-hand what happened. Frequently they are kept ignorant.

OTHER FUNCTIONS

Involve a representative from production or an engineer, as well as someone from marketing, your sponsor and the customer who has been consulted up to now. These people are essential – their role is to iron out any problems you may encounter.

FEEDBACK

If you do encounter problems, do not be defensive. Keep your mind open to corrections and modifications, and make sure these are properly entered into the system.

PRICING

Charging what the market can bear is an outdated practice. In today's climate you may wish to reach a large pool of customers quickly and go for volume; many customers buy a particular product or service if they know that others are also buying it. But you do not want to devalue your new idea by setting the price too low. Another consideration is the danger of imitation. The easier your idea is for competitors to imitate, the more difficult the pricing equation. Customers must see better value in your product or else they will go to the competitor, whether paying slightly more or less.

Your sponsor, senior management and your marketing department are wise counsel. Involve them.

POTENTIAL PARTNERS

I am an advocate of alliances and partnerships, particularly if you are working in a small organisation. They occur frequently in the IT field, with giant computer-makers tapping into – or buying – smaller software companies, and in the case of retailers who combine their wares under one roof. Such an alliance increases the marketing potential and could reduce your costs. However, there are some fundamentals to bear in mind:

- To whom will the innovation belong? Is it yours or theirs?
- Who takes responsibility for marketing? If this is not clear, efforts will quickly dwindle on both sides.
- Who will manage the alliance? How will the profits be shared? My advice is that you retain the upper hand here. People who were not involved at the start will find it difficult to manage the full implementation as you want.

→ **Try this**

→ Keep in touch with all the people who have been involved in your project, particularly if you work in an environment where people move frequently. Organise informal reunions a couple of times a year.

→ Involve marketing and production departments. Form a close relationship with their representatives.

→ Discuss with your sponsor and the marketing department your pricing strategy, but keep your options open. Ask for your customers' views.

→ Consider potential alliances. Talk to people who have entered into them. What problems did they encounter? If you decide partnership is a valid proposition, contact a potential partner and present your option as simply, clearly and unambiguously as possible. Give them time to think it over.

→ Be prepared for the fact that, even at this late stage, your innovation could fail. Nonetheless, you will have learnt an enormous amount. Keep a record.

Further resources

Drucker, Peter, *Managing for the Future*, Butterworth-Heinemann (1992), in particular Chapter 37.

Kim, W. Chan, and Renee Mauborgne, 'Knowing a Winning Business Idea When You See One', *Harvard Business Review* (September/October 2000).

Chapter 30
Leaving the comfort zone – managing change

'Change? Change? Aren't things bad enough as they are?'
– AN ENGLISH JUDGE

'Any change, even a change for the better, is always accompanied by drawbacks and discomforts.'
– ARNOLD BENNETT, NOVELIST

There are two kinds of change: change that is around us, beyond our control, and change that, through our innovation, we bring to others. They feed on each other. If you are attuned to the changes around you, you will be more likely to exploit these changes to bring a new idea about. Conversely, if you resist change or, even worse, fail to recognise it, you will become its victim. You and your company will become obsolete and your business will disappear.

Let us look at two examples:

BRITISH PUBLIC LIBRARIES

In 2002 *The Times* carried a story about public libraries, highlighting the problems and changes they faced. The headline, *'Libraries told to turn over a new leaf for survival'*, illustrated the need for every library to recognise its deficiencies, ranging from the poor quality and range of material available, restricted opening times and fierce competition with the Internet to the fact that the average age of readers was 55. All this against a background of an increasing demand for books and information and, the report claimed, the squandering of funding. If local councils ignore these signals, many public libraries will disappear. Innovative thinking is needed to turn the situation around; standing still will hasten decline, create unemployment and deprive towns of a trusted resource.

AIRLINES

How many times have you flown recently and been reminded, as you fastened your seat belt, that mobile phones must be switched off as they may interfere with the navigational system? We rely so much on the mobile phone that the instruction has become irritating. Well, not for much longer. Airlines are looking into – and some have implemented – systems that will allow the traveller – the business traveller in particular – to keep mobile phones on. Business travellers will have the opportunity of checking their e-mails and, if necessary, answering them there and then. Both Boeing and Airbus have incorporated systems in their aircraft that will not interfere with their own in-flight hardware.

LESSONS TO BE LEARNT

Here we see how, on the one hand, failure to recognise and act on signals that change is required may lead to organisations losing their effectiveness. On the other hand, recognition of change in customer habits leads to increased effectiveness.

 In practice

Change is a large subject, and there are numerous books devoted to it. But how does one begin managing it? Let me test you with some provocative statements.

First, recognise *obsolescence*.

Recognise that this wonderful new service or product you have just implemented is already yesterday's service or product. As it is born, it becomes obsolete. Can you come to terms with this concept?

Second, *implement changes when things go well*.

Imagine a situation in which your organisation is going through a difficult period – for example, a loss of market share, lower profits or a difficult merger. Would you embrace change in this situation? No. You would be suspicious that a new idea would be just one too many worry. You would not give it your best shot because you would be concerned about other priorities. Do not introduce change when people feel insecure; instead build on what they are already doing.

In contrast, imagine that your organisation is doing well: products or services are selling or being used widely, profits are as expected or targets are even being exceeded. Your colleagues are in an upbeat mood. Now is the time to drag them from their 'comfort zone'; now is the time to say 'What next?' and expect the best from them, because they have no other preoccupations. Encourage them to think beyond the comfort of today.

Do you agree? Can you do it?

INNOVATION BRINGS CHANGE TO OTHERS

If you have a new service or product you may have to demonstrate to people that adopting your idea will be an improvement on what they already have. This is a crucial part of the implementation stage, and *timing* is important. Do it too early and you may have to modify your idea, which will confuse the end-user or customer. Do it too late and people may ignore you or go for a rival solution. So how do you proceed?

 Try this

→   If you have a sponsor, use them. They will go into 'marketing mode' and use all the resources available to 'sell' your idea.

→   If you already have an end-user or customer involved, ask them to demonstrate the benefits to others.

→   Demonstrate, explain, prove to people that your idea is an improvement on what they had before. Show how *they* benefit.

→   Give people time to come to terms with their 'loss'. What you are proposing is disruptive. People need time to adapt to your vision. William Bridges offers an excellent model which acknowledges the emotional commitment involved in coming to an end (see Further Resources). Some do it quickly, others need more time.

→   Make the old obsolete. Do not allow two systems to run side by side for long. The old must be abandoned, clearly and quickly.

→   Give people the opportunity to give you feedback ... and *listen* to their comments! Modify your idea further if necessary.

Further resources

Bridges, William, *Managing Transitions*, Nicholas Brealey (1995).

Chapter 31
Widening the market – enlarging your customer base

'You cannot strengthen the weak by weakening the strong. You cannot build character by taking man's initiative. You cannot help men permanently by doing for them what they could and should do for themselves.'
– ABRAHAM LINCOLN, AMERICAN PRESIDENT

Of course, you should not wait until now to think about reaching as many customers as possible. If you prepared your innovation plan well, you will have already thought about some of these issues. Now the time is ripe to test your plan.

Innovators are not very good as this stage; they find it hard to seek out potential customers. One comforting reflection is that you are not alone – you have the help of your sponsor, who has many contacts inside and outside your organisation. And you have (or should have) your marketing department, whose job it will be to spread news of your innovation as widely as possible.

Research shows that strongly innovative companies tend to have dominance of the market, and most companies know that, if they are first in the marketplace, they will reap the largest financial reward. It follows that one factor that most companies pursue relentlessly is market share. Resist the temptation. Before you rush to reach as many customers as possible, reflect on the implications of pursuing market share single-mindedly, and consider the following:

WHICH CUSTOMERS GIVE YOU THE GREATEST VALUE?

What customer group is your innovation targeting?

Think about your business. What customers are worth cultivating? A large, prestigious customer may buy once while a smaller one may give you repeat business and loyalty, as well as propagating word-of-mouth. This customer has more worth for you.

In my business – consultancy, training and coaching – the smaller firms have remained clients for a dozen years or so. We know each other's ways, we trust each other, and if they, or I, have a new idea, we develop it together. They are well satisfied and recommend me to others. I benefit financially as I have practically no marketing costs and do not need bureaucratic procedures to tender for, or develop, something new. Some large companies manage to share this approach by reducing their procedures. In many others the formal procedures are very elaborate.

WHICH CUSTOMERS ARE STRATEGICALLY IMPORTANT?

Analyse your customers or potential customers and determine whether you can learn with and from them.

In my business, working with international business schools provides a source of learning. I meet like-minded people and, though the benefit is not financial, it is invaluable in less tangible terms. This type of client ensures that I strengthen my competencies.

HOW WILL YOUR CUSTOMERS BENEFIT FROM YOUR INNOVATION?

What are you offering that is different from what they already have? What fears do they have regarding your new product or service?

When you have gathered this information, write a brief statement to pass on to your marketing department.

INTERNAL MARKETING

After analysing which customers to target, involve your sponsor and commercial people. Your greatest asset now is your enthusiasm for your innovation, which should be contagious. Make sure, however, that they thoroughly understand your innovation, that they see the benefits and know how different your idea is from your competitors'.

USE YOUR CUSTOMERS TO MARKET YOUR INNOVATION

You can do this easily, whether you are in a small or a large firm.

- Organise an open day with those of your customers who are already using your innovation and invite a potential client to the event.
- Ask an existing customer (or user) to make a presentation about your innovation to potential customers (or users). You will be surprised and pleased by how many of them are prepared to do this.
- If needed, plan training sessions to help customers

make the mental leap required for them to adopt your innovation.

 In practice

→ If you want to strengthen your long-term relationships with your customers, you need to consider their worth to you and your organisation. Customers are not necessarily equal.

→ Aim at a specific market, not everyone indiscriminately.

→ Market with and to people who understand your innovation.

→ Help potential customers adapt their mindset to yours so that they will be persuaded to embrace your idea.

Case study

I once made the mistake of not ensuring that a client thoroughly understood what I was doing. Some years ago a fairly large training company offered to sell some of my products, but none of their marketing people had direct experience of what I did and I did not go to talk to them personally. There were hardly any sales. Subsequently a project came up with a very prestigious client, and I suggested to the managing director of the training company that we both go and see them. After the meeting with the customer the MD exclaimed, 'I had no idea of the type of work you do. It is all very deep stuff!' I got the job. (That, by the way, was one of the starting points for this book.)

Further resources

Hope, Jeremy and Tony, *Competing in the Third Wave*, Harvard
  Business School Press (1997), in particular Chapter 2.

Chapter 32
Know your enemy – keeping competitors at bay

'Competition is healthy, maybe even essential, but there has to be more to life than winning or we should nearly all be losers.'
– CHARLES HANDY, MANAGEMENT SPECIALIST

In business (and increasingly in the public sector) people question the way they do things by looking at and analysing how their competitors are operating. Techniques like benchmarking are geared to give an accurate measurement of how your organisation is performing when compared to others in the same sector or field. But how does one translate the analysis into action?

Before, during and after the launch of your innovation, you need to keep competitors at arm's length, at least. This means understanding your competitors' services or products.

1 INFORM YOUR PEOPLE OF THE COMPETITION

Many, if not most, organisations gather data about their competitors. Yet, in most cases, this data is not shared with the marketing people or the production department; rather the information is kept to board members and the analysts who compile the information. Why? If you really want people to improve, you need to give them the reasons why they need to improve.

Specific performance or productivity results are generally not released freely within organisations. In the best cases, graphs are pinned to walls highlighting comparative productivity levels *between plants*, but not *as compared with competitors' plants*.

If managers believe that competition within the firm is a good thing (and they must, otherwise why do they pin up these internal results?), is it not equally essential to understand the external competition that could threaten one's business?

2 KNOW YOUR CUSTOMER'S PRODUCTS OR SERVICES

Stories about the Japanese technique of getting hold of a Western product and disassembling it are now part of business folklore. But why not emulate it? How can you think of improving on what is already on the market if you do not know these products inside and out?

I often suggest this procedure to my clients when appropriate, and I continue to be amazed that they are not doing it as a matter of course. Besides giving your engineers and marketing people ideas on how to improve what they are looking at, it is also invaluable experience for a young trainee. He or she will understand design weaknesses better, and will be imbued early on with a sense of purpose: to do better.

3 TALK TO YOUR COMPETITORS' CUSTOMERS

Perhaps your commercial people already do, but how do they use the information? There is a lot to be discovered that could be immensely helpful. Why do these potential clients go elsewhere? Is it location, pricing, after-sales service care, quality, ignorance of other similar products? Develop a rigorous feedback mechanism to get hold of this information.

4 AVOID THE QUICK FIX

If you really want to get ahead of your competitors, you need to adopt a long-term strategic stance. The short-termism of much of the Anglo-Saxon mentality is a recipe for failure – certainly in terms of innovation. Problems are poorly defined; people are kept busy with procedures and specific tasks and are not given time to think; financial results at the end of each week, month or year take precedence over increasing market share and responding to customer needs. Such short-sightedness is self-destructive. Examples that have led to the demise of organisations or even a whole industry abound.

- The loss of the motorcycle industry in Britain
- The difficulties of the motor industry in the USA in the face of growing Japanese competition
- The demise of the GEC/Marconi empire
- The collapse of the merchant bank Barings

Obviously other factors are involved in the failure of these organisations and industries. But if the CEOs had kept long-term survival firmly in mind their management priorities and decisions would have been quite different.

In general, continental European and Asian businesses are much better at taking a long-term view. And it is the long-term view which ensures continued success.

5 AVOID COMPLACENCY

Do not be tempted to think that your product or service is truly unique and ahead of the competition. This is dangerous. All products and services eventually compete. Do not rest now: think of the next step, the next improvement, the next gap in the market.

 In practice

- ➜ Publicise widely within your organisation the data you have on competitors and discuss its implications.
- ➜ Organise discussions to see whether ideas from elsewhere could be adapted and improved.
- ➜ Encourage people to think ahead, to think strategically. If your innovation is about to be launched, what will you eventually replace it with? Your service or product is obsolete as soon as it reaches the marketplace. So what next? Let your customers know that you understand that your innovation is not an end in itself.
- ➜ If you are working in a university or school, find out how other teaching institutions are organised in terms of research. Ask a newly appointed lecturer or teacher to visit an institution similar to your own and make a presentation of their findings to your staff.

Further resources

Lawler, Edward E., III, *From the Ground Up*, Jossey-Bass Publishers (1996), in particular Chapters 10 and 11.

Nadler, Gerald, and Shozo Hibino, *Breakthrough Thinking*, Prima Publishing (1990), in particular Chapter 12.

Rydz, John S., *Managing Innovation*, Ballinger Publishing (1986), in particular Chapter 5.

Chapter 33

Know your limits – can the idea be developed further?

'Le mieux est l'ennemi du bien (The best is the enemy of the good).'
– VOLTAIRE, ENLIGHTENMENT AUTHOR

'Who the hell wants to hear actors talk?'
– JACK WARNER, IN 1922, QUESTIONING THE NEED TO MOVE FROM SILENT MOVIES

Do you know your limits? Do you know when to stop, when to go on? These questions can be dealt with at both micro and macro levels. At a micro level, these questions are addressed to you, the innovator; at the macro level, they are for the senior management of organisations.

THE MICRO LEVEL

There comes a time when you need to compromise. You cannot go on improving your idea for ever. Why? Because your resources are dwindling and your customers will lose interest and go elsewhere. A sense of urgency must prevail to the end. In short, perfectionism is costly and unnecessary. Remember the Pareto Principle: for many endeavours 20 per cent of the effort gains 80 per cent of the target. It is the final 20 per cent, perfection, which is really costly.

Keep in mind that your starting point was an opportunity that you spotted first. Opportunities do not last for ever; avoid the distraction of perfection. It is more worthwhile to get your innovation 'out there', test it, then modify it if it needs improvement.

People who have a tendency towards perfection forget the value of excellence. In innovation excellence is your aim: to implement your idea within budget, on time, and to the satisfaction of your end-users. Occasionally this attitude requires humility!

THE MACRO LEVEL

Innovations start their decline as soon as they are born. It is the concern of senior management to think about how a new product or service will eventually be replaced. So here we go beyond the Japanese ethos of *kaizen*, continuous improvement. While instilling a culture of continuous improvement is necessary in organisations, I am talking here about putting in place mechanisms that will help your people to come up time and again with new products or services that are needed in the marketplace. Thus you and your organisation need to have the courage to challenge and change established approaches. This is not easy, and it will not happen unless the top management seeks out, and implements, ways to help their personnel to accept discontinuity; or, even better, to anticipate discontinuity.

Senior managers who do not understand the inevitability of obsolescence and discontinuity will hang on to ongoing business. By hanging on they will not hear their colleagues' ideas, they will not see opportunities, and they will demotivate those who do. They fear that their present success coming to an end will leave them with a vacuum. They mistrust new ideas.

SEPARATE ORGANISATIONS

If you have a fair number of managers who would rather manage what they have than encourage their teams to innovate, then do not exhort them to produce new ideas and projects. This is not their '*métier*'. You need to make a clear distinction between those who thrive on change and those who do not. Separate them, with different budgets, minimum bureaucracy, and direct access to senior management. In short, you need separate organisations, or businesses, working in parallel but with very different aims. The function of one is to keep the business going today, of the other to ensure that the business survives and is renewed for the future.

 Try this

→ As an innovator, learn when further development of your innovation becomes detrimental, when the extra effort it requires is too costly.

→ As the sponsor or senior manager, keep your eye on the last stages of implementation and, if necessary, push your team to finish the project. Hold discussions with the team and the main customer and demonstrate that you have all reached the last hurdle. And jump over it!

→ Ask your successful innovative team, 'What next?'

→ With your innovative people, list the various approaches you could use to replace products or services.

→ Forecast the limitations of your new product or service, plotted against current trends.

→   Reorganise your department or organisation with autonomous teams whose job it is to challenge the present and secure the future.

Further resources

Foster, Richard, *Innovation*, Summit Books (1986), in particular the Epilogue and Appendices.

Chapter 34
Moving forward – learning from mistakes

*'Show me a person who has never made a mistake and
I'll show you somebody who has never achieved much.'*
– JOAN COLLINS, ACTRESS

*'Leaders are learners. They learn from their mistakes as
well as their successes.'*
– JAMES KOUZES AND BARRY POSNER, LEADERSHIP
MANAGEMENT CONSULTANTS

*'Never believe in faith, see for yourself. What you yourself
don't learn, you don't know.'*
– BERTOLD BRECHT, PLAYWRIGHT

'The real fault is to have faults and not amend them.'
– CONFUCIUS, CHINESE PHILOSOPHER

Remember that innovation does not happen in a risk-free
environment and mistakes will be made. This chapter will
help you conduct learning reviews (often with your
customer) and understand how often we prevent ourselves
from learning from our mistakes and those of others.

Once we become conscious of how we think and interact we develop the ability to think differently. This is

particularly relevant when things do not turn out the way we anticipated.

1 BUILD A LEARNING ORGANISATION

- *Do you have regular progress reviews with your team?* Consider whether you test your experiences regularly; that is, your successes as well as your failures. Does this mean you have structures designed to allow reflection?
- *When was a mistake picked up? What was learnt?* Consider whether you have the capability for effective remedial action.
- *How are the lessons learnt disseminated through your organisation?*
  Are the lessons shared with everyone? Or are they hidden within a blame culture? '*A little learning is a dangerous thing,*' wrote Alexander Pope. Quite.

2 LEARN FROM CRITICAL INCIDENTS

Set up ad hoc reviews of significant incidents. Successes must not be inflated, failures and mistakes must not be ignored. These are special learning opportunities. If these incidents are not considered carefully the same opportunities may be missed or blunders may be repeated. Ask yourself:

- What happened, how and why?
- How can this be repeated or avoided in the future?
- How can we ensure that we have learnt from this incident?

3 USE WHAT YOU HAVE LEARNED

- Compile a report detailing all key learning issues

- Make it available in your organisation's library and accessible to all other staff members.

→ **In practice**

At an individual level I have found Peter Honey and Alan Mumford's work on learning styles (see Further Resources) invaluable. The authors remind us that people learn naturally in several different styles.

Some people learn from *doing things*; the authors call such people *Activists*. They initiate and perform tasks, they like to experiment.

Others *reflect*. They watch others' activities and reach decisions in their own time.

Some are *Theorists*. They learn best with a model, a framework, a concept or theory. They read, analyse and understand complex situations through intellectual engagement.

And another category of people learn from linking theory to actual problems. They are *Pragmatists*. They enjoy techniques that relate directly to their own problems.

Which descriptions strike a chord with you? Can you also recognise how your own team members learn best? If you can, then your learning programme needs to take their styles into account as well if it is to make any impact.

Further resources

Honey, Peter, and Alan Mumford, *Learning Styles* (1983) and *Manual of Learning Opportunities*.

Pedlar, Mike, John Burgoyne and Tom Boydell, *The Learning Company, A Strategy for Sustainable Development*, McGraw-Hill (1991).

Senge, Peter, *The Fifth Discipline Fieldbook*, Nicholas Brealey (1994).

Chapter 35
And finally ... celebrate!

'As for the best leaders, the people do not notice their existence. The next best, the people honour and praise. The next, the people fear; and the next, the people hate. When the best leader's work is done, the people say, "We did it ourselves".'
– LAO-TZU, CHINESE PHILOSOPHER

If you have reached this stage, well done! Take the time to mark the occasion. Celebration is not a reward; it is the spontaneous acknowledgement of a shared experience, commitment and success. It is the recognition of the investment people have made in the project and, conversely, the investment the organisation has made in its people.

Celebration is almost a tribal ceremony, a banquet or party where all participants are treated as equals. The covert benefits are a bonding of people who have lived through a unique set of circumstances, who have learnt together the art of survival and who have overcome.

In our Western society, pressed for time, we neglect celebrations. But they are a significant rite of passage and, in itself, a celebration is also a learning step, an official ending.

In practice

Celebration works best if:

→ You limit the guests to the innovative team. This can include the major customer and the sponsor, but leave senior management out.

→ It is organised around an away-day – say going to a golf club or a hotel with sports facilities, or

→ An evening in an unusual venue: a restaurant with exotic food, for example.

→ The day, or evening, is organised soon after the successful launch, before the team is disbanded and preoccupied with other interests.

→ Others in your organisation know that you are celebrating.

The benefits are, I think, clear:

→ People feel valued

→ They formally finish the project on a 'high'

→ The concepts of fun and work become linked

→ The bonding of like-minded people is reinforced – and thus can be replicated

Further resources

There is not much available on this subject, which shows how neglected the issue is, but Rosabeth Moss-Kanter alludes to it in *The Change Masters*, Unwin (1983).

Conclusion:
Innovation and its place in the work environment

Throughout this book, I have tried to demystify innovation. The process is easy to grasp: what it requires is the will and discipline to make it happen. In commercial organisations or public sector institutions innovation does not occur by accident or erratically. It only happens when

- People purposefully pursue business opportunities
- The same people are supported by core competencies
- They are driven by a desire to succeed

To recognise business opportunities the organisation (that is, senior management) must be outward looking. Too frequently senior managers are engrossed in internal turmoil or else satisfied with present results with little concern for tomorrow. Unless they realise how crucial their role is, I see little chance of progress.

So, as a senior manager, what can you do?

- Boost your employees' skills
- Give them assignments that will develop their creative abilities
- Give them the autonomy to pursue ideas, with adequate resources: time and a modest budget
- Offer the knowledge of more senior managers to sponsor projects

- Tell your people that they matter

The same applies in public institutions. I work with many British universities and government ministries, in which people interact and work to have an impact and make a contribution to the society in which they live – the ideal ingredients for innovation! Yet how often do we hear of a vice-chancellor or a head of department or a permanent secretary getting their people together and asking, 'What opportunities are there for us to give a better service to our students or taxpayers?', 'What improvements could we make to what we deliver?', 'What and where are our strengths? How could we extend or build on what we have?' or 'What threats are there to our university/department/ministry?'

I have been privileged to know two such persons – a principal in academia and a permanent secretary, now retired, whose successful battles against red tape became legendary. But why are these examples not universal? These institutions need to renew themselves if they are to survive and thrive in the years to come. They need to be imbued with an innovative spirit and attract innovators.

You may have noticed that the word 'profits' does not figure much in this book, although 'success' does. A paradox? I do not think so. I believe that successful organisations are not focused solely on profits; they are motivated by a desire to produce something useful and, in time, to follow it with something else useful. Of course, that something has to make a profit. But profit is not the end, it is a means. Success is the end, and where there is success, money follows.

Turning your organisation into an innovative one will lead you to success.

Index of citations and references

Subject index

Piatkus Business Books

Piatkus Business Books have been created for people like
you, whether you are busy executives and managers or just
starting your career. They provide expert knowledge in a
clear and easy-to-follow format. All the books are written
by specialists in their field. They will help you improve your
skills quickly and effortlessly in the workplace and on a
personal level. They are available in all good bookshops or
by visiting our website at www.piatkus.co.uk

**The 10-Day MBA: A step-by-step guide to mastering the
skills taught in top business schools** Steven Silbiger

**10-Minute Time And Stress Management: How to gain an
'extra' 10 hours a week!** Dr David Lewis

**BodyTalk at Work: How to use effective body language to
boost your career** Judi James

Brain Power: The 12-week mental training programme
Marilyn vos Savant & Leonore Fleischer

Careershift: How to plan and develop a successful career
Bridget Wright

**The Complete Book of Business Etiquette: The essential
guide to getting ahead in business** Lynne Brennan &
David Block

The Complete Conference Organisers Handbook Robin
Connor

**The Complete Time Management System: Change the way
you work and 'save' 2 hours a day!** Christian H. Godefroy
& John Clark

**Confident Public Speaking: How to communicate
successfully using the PowerTalk system** Christian
Godefroy & Stephanie Barrat

**Continuous Quality Improvement: A hands-on guide to
setting up and sustaining a cost-effective quality
programme** Alasdair White

Corporate Charisma: How to achieve world-class

recognition by maximising your company's image, brands and culture Dr Paul Temporal & Dr Harry Alder

Dealing With Difficult People: Proven strategies for handling stressful situations and defusing tensions Roberta Cava

Digital Aboriginal: Radical business strategies for a world without rules Mikela Tarlow

The Engaged Customer: The new rules of Internet Direct Marketing Hans Peter Brondmo

Enterprise One to One: Tools for building unbreakable customer relationships in the information age Don Peppers & Martha Rogers

The Essential Guide to Developing Your Staff: How to recruit, train coach and mentor top-quality people Alasdair White

Fierce Conversations: Achieving success in work and in life, one conversation at a time Susan Scott

Financial Know-how for Non-financial Managers: Easy ways to understand accounts and financial planning John Spencer and Adrian Pruss

Getting Everything You Can Out of All You've Got: 21 ways you can out-think, out-perform and out-earn the competition Jay Abraham

Getting Things Done: How to achieve stress-free productivity David Allen

Grow Rich with peace of mind Napoleon Hill

How to Survive Without a Job: Practical solutions for developing skills and building self-esteem Ursula Markham

How to Win a Lot More Business in a Lot Less Time: The 10 commandments of speed Michael LeBoeuf

Intellectual Capital: The proven way to establish your company's real value by measuring its hidden brainpower Leif Edvinsson & Michael S. Malone

Interviewing Skills for Managers Tony & Gillian Pont

Life Coaching for Work: The formula for happiness and success at work Eileen Mulligan

Mind Power: How to use positive thinking to change your life Christian Godefroy & D. R. Steevens

More Time, Less Stress: How to create two extra hours every day Judi James

Napoleon Hill's Keys to Positive Thinking: 10 steps to health, wealth and success Napoleon Hill

Napoleon Hill's Keys to Success Napoleon Hill (ed. Matthew Sartwell)

Napoleon Hill's Positive Action Plan: How to make every day a success Napoleon Hill

Napoleon Hill's Unlimited Success: 52 steps to personal and financial reward Napoleon Hill (ed. Matthew Sartwell)

Network Your Way to Success: Discover the secrets of the world's top connectors John Timperley

NLP For Managers: How to achieve excellence at work Dr Harry Alder

NLP in 21 Days: A complete introduction Dr Harry Alder & Beryl Heather

NLP: The new art and science of getting what you want Dr Harry Alder

The One to One Future: Building business relationships one customer at a time Don Peppers & Martha Roger

The Outstanding Negotiator: How to develop your arguing power Christian Godefroy & Luis Robert

The Perfect CV: How to get the job you really want Tom Jackson

The Perfect Store: Inside eBay Adam Cohen

Professional Network Marketing: Practical advice for building a successful network Bobbi DePorter & Mike Hernacki

Quantum Learning for Business: Discover how to be more effective, confident and successful at work Bobbi DePorter with Mike Hernacki